TRUE STORIES FROM THE FILES OF THE FBI

TRUE STORIES
FROM THE FILES OF THE FBI

W. Cleon Skousen

IZZARD INK LLC

Published by Izzard Ink LLC.

Find True Stories from the Files of the FBI on Facebook:

http://www.facebook.com/FBITrueStories

To contact W. Cleon Skousen about bulk orders please e-mail info@wcleonskousen.com.

Published by:

Izzard Ink, LLC
PO Box 522251
Salt Lake City, Utah 84109

Second Edition: October 2014

Hardback ISBN: 978-1630720803
Paperback ISBN: 978-1630720636
eBook ISBN: 978-1630720599

Book design by Glen M. Edelstein
Cover design by Glen M. Edelstein

TRUE STORIES FROM THE FILES OF THE FBI

Contents

Foreword

With the end of World War II, FBI Director J. Edgar Hoover saw that another war was just beginning. This one would be tougher, more political, harder to handle, and would require the best his Bureau could offer.

With FBI agents already scattered coast to coast in 1945, tracing down infiltrators and espionage spies from foreign enemies, Hoover had been tracking the development of a new threat to America—an enemy that rode in on the heels of "dumbing down" the American public and presenting itself as the new benign, fair, and friendly road to change.

It was called communism, a movement to overthrow the Constitution and the American way of life. Hoover saw these ideas beginning to infiltrate America's most respected institutions. It was the worst kind of enemy because this one was home-grown.

When World War II ended, Hoover's secret files were already overflowing with damning evidence of personal moral corruption and ulterior motives by names and faces familiar to most post-war Americans—people already respected as heroes or friends to the war's great cause. But Hoover knew better. He had the proof.

He knew by holding tight to those records, the worst elements in the inner circles of American power politics would be kept back.

He also knew that one skipped heart beat or "accidental" car crash on the way to work was all it would take for his office to be emptied out and those files to quickly disappear.

Hoover loved America. He was married to his job and hung on to it through political pressures and assassination attempts for many years beyond his normal retirement age. Even after his death, his reputation and personal character were of such high esteem and influence that his many enemies sought to bury even the memory of the man. They tried to assassinate his reputation with scurrilous lies and innuendo.

But at the end of World War II, those events were still in the future, and Hoover saw the critical need to alert the rising generation about the coming plague. He took several steps to educate the baby-boomers and their parents about the dangers of malaise and detachment from their sentry duty over America's heart and soul.

One of Hoover's early projects was a descriptive report on what the FBI was, what it could do, why it existed, and its role in the safety and security of America. He wanted to teach the youth in particular that it was their job "to clean up America."

Tasked to write that report was 32-year-old FBI agent W. Cleon Skousen.

By this time Skousen had proven himself to be one of the Bureau's promising public speakers and writers. He was already a published author, and was giving 100-200 speeches a year.

Skousen was given access to the FBI files for his research. His finished product was called "The Story of the Federal Bureau of Investigation," published in 1945. It was subsequently reprinted millions of times and distributed over a period of several years.

Those true stories related in this publication are as close to re-enactments of actual events as mere words can create. It was a time in America's history when roving gangs with machine guns mowed down rival gangs and innocent bystanders to control territories and illicit activities. Many bragged of the carved notches in the wooden stock of their weapons, tally marks of another life taken. The biggest prize of all was gunning down a police officer or even better, an agent from the FBI.

From a time that lives on for most people in old black-and-white "shoot 'em up" Hollywood movies, and the more dramatic portrayals by special effects teams using full-color digitization, the era of the gangster still reverberates through American culture with an almost romantic affixation to those bloody, gun-smoke days of old.

"True Stories from the Files of the FBI" is not pulp fiction or dramatized back alley stick-ups. It's the real thing, presented for a generation of Americans who today have the mandate on their shoulders to "clean up America."

PAUL B. SKOUSEN
June 10, 2014
Salt Lake City, Utah

INTRODUCTION TO THE FBI

"Wanted by the FBI!"

Those words caught the attention of a Midwestern schoolboy waiting for his father to complete some business in the Sheriff's Office of their home county. The youngster noticed something familiar about the fugitive whose picture appeared under those striking words. Then he realized suddenly that the man described by the Federal Bureau of Investigation as an armed robber had worked on his own father's farm until a short time before.

Special Agents of the FBI were advised. They quickly traced the fugitive and, with the help of local officers, took him into custody. The wanted man, who had been in hiding for a year, was tried, convicted, and sentenced to serve 25 years in prison.

That was democracy's answer to a man who would not follow the rules. The FBI acted for the people of the United States, who are firm in their determination to preserve law and order. The alert youngster is typical of thousands of Americans who respect the law and furnish invaluable information to Special Agents of the FBI every day.

The Federal Bureau of Investigation is the investigative arm of the United States Department of Justice, headed by the Attorney General, who is the chief legal officer of the United States.

The functions of the FBI are two-fold. As a fact-finding agency, it investigates violations of federal laws and presents its findings to the Attorney General, his assistants and the United States Attorneys who decide whether the people involved are to be brought to trial. As a service agency, it assists law enforcement in identification and technical matters.

To do the work, the FBI has Special Agents assigned to 56 field divisions throughout the United States and in Puerto Rico, Alaska and Hawaii. Each of these divisions is under a Special Agent in Charge (SAC) who reports to the Director in Washington, D.C. Within an hour a Special Agent can arrive at practically any point in the country where his services may be needed.

To tell the story of the FBI is to recite the history of men and women seeking to make America more secure. It is the story of a long line of Presidents, Attorneys General, members of Congress, and millions of honest, loyal citizens who form a solid front against crime.

Special Agents in a two-way radio car.

"G-MEN"

In the early morning hours of September 26, 1933, a small group of men surrounded a house in Memphis, Tennessee. In the house was George "Machine-Gun" Kelly, graduate of Leavenworth Penitentiary. He was wanted by the FBI for kidnapping. For two months FBI Agents had trailed the gangster and his wife, Kathryn Kelly. Quickly the men of the FBI, accompanied by local law enforcement officers, closed in around the house and entered.

"We are Federal officers.... Come out with your hands up...."

"Machine-Gun" Kelly stood cowering in a corner. His heavy face twitched as he gazed at the men before him. Reaching trembling hands up towards the ceiling he whimpered, "Don't shoot, G-Men, don't shoot!"

That was the beginning of a new name for FBI Agents. By the time Kelly had been convicted and had received his sentence of life imprisonment, the new nickname, an abbreviation of "Government Men," had taken hold throughout the underworld. Along the grapevine of the powerful empire of crime passed whispered words of warning about the "G-Men."

G-men handcuffing a fugitive.

WAR AGAINST THE UNDERWORLD

"Machine-Gun" Kelly was a product of the wave of lawlessness which swept over the nation in the early '30s. Kidnapping, murder, bank robbery and many other crimes of violence occurred daily. Dangerous outlaws enlisted the petty thief, the small-fry hoodlum, and the ex-convict to form powerful gangs. Professional killers were hired to eliminate honest law enforcement officers, civic-minded citizens and members of rival gangs. Shady characters willing to provide temporary shelter for gangsters in the larger cities joined up. Bullet-proof vests, stolen sub-machine guns and high-powered "getaway cars" were rated as necessary equipment.

To check this wave of lawlessness and bring security to the nation, Congress swiftly passed many new laws to increase the authority of the Federal Bureau of Investigation. In 1932, the Federal Kidnapping Statute making it a crime to take kidnapped persons from one state to another was passed. During the following year, the FBI solved every kidnapping case referred to it. Among these were the Cannon, Ottley, Urschel, Boettcher, Luer, McElroy, Hart, Bremer and Hamm kidnappings in which ransom demands totaled $782,000.

Next came the Federal Extortion Act by which the writer of a threatening letter could be put in prison for as long as 20 years and fined $5,000.

Bank robberies by notorious gangsters on a nationwide basis were met with the Federal Bank Robbery Act, which now extends its protection to National banks, Federal Reserve banks and banks whose deposits are insured by the government.

In 1934, Congress had finished the task of building the FBI into the general investigative agency of the Federal Government. In the same year additional duties were assigned. The Federal Reward Bill authorized payment of as much as $25,000 to persons helping to capture dangerous criminals or giving information leading to their arrests. The National Stolen Property Act made it a crime to take forged and counterfeit securities or stolen property valued at $5,000 or more from one state to another. The Federal Anti-Racketeering Statute made it unlawful to interfere with trade between states by force or violence. The Unlawful Flight to Avoid Prosecution Statute made it a Federal offense for persons to flee from one state to another to avoid prosecution for certain serious crimes or to avoid testifying in court in important criminal cases. In the years that have followed, other laws have been passed designed to better protect the citizens of the United States. Now the FBI is responsible for the investigation of violations of more than 100 Federal statutes ranging from bankruptcy to treason.

ORIGIN OF THE FBI

Although the FBI did not become well known until after the great crime wave of the '30s, the organization was in existence many years before.

The FBI dates back to 1908, when Attorney General Charles Bonaparte directed that Department of Justice investigations be handled by a small group of special investigators. In the following year the name "Bureau of Investigation" was assigned to this group.

The small organization gradually grew during the succeeding years. The Selective Service Act of World War I and espionage laws to block the work of spies brought new duties. Then the National Motor Vehicle Theft Act was passed in 1919 to curb the increasing transportation of stolen automobiles from state to state.

In 1924, Attorney General Harlan F. Stone, who later became Chief Justice of the Supreme Court of the United States, appointed J. Edgar Hoover, then 29 years of age, as Director of the Bureau. He accepted with the understanding that henceforth this organization was to be a career service in which ability and good character were to be the requirements for appointment with performance and achievement the only grounds for promotion.

YOUTH AND SCIENCE TAKE OVER

The new Director knew it would take years to build the FBI into a streamlined, investigative machine to fight crime. New requirements for appointment as a Special Agent were set up, providing for college men trained in law and accounting. To be eligible the applicant had to be between the ages of 23 and 35 and physically fit. Each applicant was thoroughly investigated before appointment. His school record and every activity were searched for flaws in his honesty or ability.

Gradually the new organization began to take form. Congress approved the transfer of fingerprints at Leavenworth Penitentiary and the criminal records maintained by the International Association of Chiefs of Police to the FBI. Thus began what is now known as the Integrated Automated Fingerprint Identification System. Thanks to the cooperation of national and international law enforcement organizations the original collection of 810,188 fingerprints has multiplied to 70 million prints in the criminal master file along with an additional 250 million civil prints.

Training schools for Special Agents and Accountants were started in Washington to equip future G-Men with modern crime-detection methods. These offer courses in federal law, accounting, fingerprint science, crime scene searches, interviews, photography, firearms and jujitsu.

A crime-detection laboratory was established to make examinations for the FBI and to serve as a scientific clearing house for evidence and crime problems submitted by police and sheriffs throughout the country.

CRIME MEETS ITS MATCH

By 1934 the gangs had discovered that the rich days of the underworld empire were passing. One by one the gangland bosses were being given new forwarding addresses: prisons at Alcatraz, Atlanta and Leavenworth. Backed by cooperating local officers and an aroused public, the FBI was sweeping the alleys of the underworld.

Newspapers headlined the violent deaths of "public enemies" who chose to fight it out rather than surrender:

On July 22, 1934, John Dillinger was killed on a Chicago street while resisting arrest. On October 22, 1934, "Pretty Boy" Floyd met death on an Ohio farm while resisting Federal arrest. On November 27, 1934, "Baby Face" Nelson, murderer of three FBI Agents, was mortally wounded in a gun battle on an Illinois highway while resisting arrest. On January 8, 1935, Russell Gibson, member of the powerful Barker-Karpis Gang, fell under a hail of lead in a Chicago alley after he had fired at a Special Agent who demanded his surrender. On January 16, 1935, "Ma" and Fred Barker, leaders of the Barker-Karpis Gang who were hiding out in a Florida cottage, answered Agents' demand for surrender with bursts from Thompson sub-machine guns. The Barkers were killed in the gun battle.

On October 12, 1937, G-Men were fired upon by members of the Brady Gang at Bangor, Maine. An FBI Agent was wounded but Alfred Brady and Clarence Shaffer were killed and the gang smashed. On October 7, 1938, Adam Richetti was executed in connection with the slaying of four law enforcement officers, including an FBI Agent, in the "Kansas City Massacre." Vernon Miller, also wanted for the same crime, was clubbed and shot to death by underworld "pals" who by that time considered a Federal fugitive of his type too dangerous to have around.

In the desperate war with the gang trigger men, several FBI Agents lost their lives. But the fearlessness of the Agents in gun battles and their straight shooting soon caused the word to be passed in underworld circles that it didn't pay to "shoot it out" with G-Men.

Within three years after the FBI received general investigative jurisdiction over Federal crimes, 11,153 persons had been arrested and the Bund (a pro-Nazi organization in the 1930s) prepared to go underground. The Japanese spies who laced their network of intrigue back and forth across the West Coast from Shinto Temples to dock dives, became less bold in their prowling around military and naval bases.

Important information had come to light. There was a fantastic Nazi plot to grab the secret plans for the defense of the East Coast of the United States by luring a high-ranking American Army officer to a New York hotel room, overpowering him and seizing the papers. There was a plot to get confidential codes and maps of the United States Army Air Corps and complete blueprints of the newest aircraft carriers, the Enterprise and the Yorktown. And then on Valentine's Day, 1939, a spy made an attempt to secure 35 blank American passports by impersonating an official in the Department of State. That spy was Guenther Gustav Maria Rumrich, and his arrest followed immediately after. When brought to trial, Rumrich, Hoffman, Voss and Glaser were convicted. But the penalties were light. This was "peacetime" espionage, and the sentences for all four spies totaled 14 years.

It was soon apparent that the most effective way to counter-spy was to check the movements of prying enemy agents. Little was accomplished by arresting spies after their damaging work had been done. As later developments proved, it was necessary to know the innermost workings of enemy espionage—the extent of their networks, their plans for causing damage in our country through sabotage, their interest in certain highly confidential military information. Enemy espionage not only required detection, it had to be prevented.

Franklin D. Roosevelt, recognizing the dangers ahead, undertook in the early summer of 1939 to prevent the confusion of World War I, when more than 20 agencies investigated the activities of spies and saboteurs. He designated the FBI as the clearing house and coordinating agency for all matters bearing on our internal security.

FBI Agents received instructions to survey over 2,500 industrial plants which were beginning to pour out the implements of war. Other Agents gathered and wove the threads of enemy espionage together—the German spies were making a last desperate effort to entrench themselves before the shooting war began.

Then on Sunday morning, September 1, 1939, the powder keg exploded. Germany smashed into Poland with planes, tanks, mobile artillery and thousands of highly trained troops. The whole world was startled.

A General Intelligence Conference was created with the heads of Military and Naval Intelligence Divisions and the FBI empowered to establish procedures on how best to protect America. Weekly conferences were held by executives of the three intelligence agencies. Police Conferences were held throughout the nation to unite the entire law enforcement front for the showdown. The survey of war plants sped up. Specialized training in counter-spying and counter-sabotage was ordered for all FBI Agents. More FBI men and more equipment were authorized by Congress. The public was urged to cooperate in every possible way.

Hidden camera shooting through a two-way mirror
photographing spy ring members.

BREAKING OF THE LARGEST SPY RING
IN U.S. HISTORY

Previously, the Nazis had thrown their largest American spy ring into action. The Nazis sneered at the "weakness" of democracy and boasted of the security they had built up around their own spy network; they were ready for anything.

The paymaster for this ring was "Harry Sawyer," a naturalized American who went to Germany to visit his mother. Major Nicholaus Adolf Fritz Ritter of the German Espionage Service forced him to become a German spy. He was trained in the espionage school in Hamburg. He studied photography, secret writing and the Nazi technique of collecting data. Last of all, he was given a thousand dollars, numerous addresses, the blessings of the Nazis and a ticket to New York.

As he embarked for America, "Harry Sawyer" carried in his watch a quantity of stamp-sized microphotographs bearing secret operating orders. He was to use a small camera for taking pictures, build a short-wave radio station to communicate with Hamburg and join the National Guard to secure military information.

"Sawyer" landed in New York and was met at the docks by

two men who drove him to a hotel for a brief conference. Later, he cabled Hamburg: "Arrived safe. Had pleasant trip." This prearranged message meant he was safely settled and prepared to go to work.

He neglected to mention that he was now working for the FBI, that he had never intended to "sell out" the United States, and that he had reported fully on his contacts with the Germans.

"Sawyer" carried out the instructions of his Nazi masters, made the requested contacts, paid out the money. Slowly the network of the spy ring unfolded. New agents and various "contacts" were revealed. A shortwave transmitting station was built and was operated continuously by undercover Agents of the FBI. More than 500 messages passed back and forth across the Atlantic, but important details were cut out by the Army and Navy, which worked closely with the FBI.

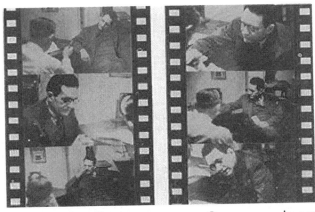

Frederick Joubert Duquesne, master German spy, in actual photographs taken by a concealed FBI camera.

Frederick Joubert Duquesne, a professional German spy for forty years, boasted to "Sawyer" of his ability to fool the FBI. From his sock he pulled out blueprints on the new M-1 rifle, torpedo boats, secret plane plans. Hidden FBI motion picture cameras photographed him as he did so. He waved his arms jubilantly as he gloated over the success of his large espionage ring.

In Europe the war of nerves had changed to a "shooting" war. Germany and her allies had begun their conquests. FBI officials considered it a good time to smash the Duquesne ring, the backbone of the Nazi Espionage Service in the United States.

On the weekend of June 28, 1941, the FBI arrested the spies whose every move had been followed for nearly two years. Thirty-three German agents, including Duquesne, were brought in. Several were American-born.

Nineteen members of the ring pleaded guilty. The other fourteen stood trial and were found guilty by a jury on December 15, 1941. On January 2, 1942, the group received total sentences exceeding 520 years in prison and fines amounting to $18,000.

But this was still "peacetime espionage."

The full force of war had not yet hit America. But the collapse of the Duquesne ring caused all other Nazi agents to work feverishly, as though American planes were already bombarding the Reich. From Germany came the order: "Under no circumstances attract the attention of the FBI!"

THE KURT LUDWIG CASE

Back in March, 1941, a tall, middle-aged man wearing horn-rimmed glasses and carrying a brown brief case was knocked down and killed by a New York taxicab. Amazed spectators saw his companion reach down quickly, grab a brief case and disappear in the crowd.

The traffic victim was "Julio Lopez Lido," apparently a Spanish subject. His unclaimed body was buried by the Spanish Consulate.

FBI Agents were keenly interested in "Julio Lopez Lido." He was not a Spanish subject. He was a German—Captain Ulrich von der Osten, Nazi army officer who entered the United States via Japan to direct one of the cells of Nazi espionage. The companion who had been so anxious to get away from the accident turned out to be Kurt Frederick Ludwig, an Ohio-born, German-reared, leather goods merchant.

Working in the background, the FBI found that Ludwig was extremely active in the United States as a German espionage agent. In fact, he stepped into the shoes of Captain von der Osten and took over control of the latter's spy ring. Friends of Ludwig said he once stood in high favor with Adolf Hitler; that he had been with Hitler in the Munich Beer Hall Putsch before the Nazi rise to power.

Ludwig purchased expensive radio equipment and took a course at a radio school. He sent numerous packages to Germany. He kept in constant contact with the Bund and recruited his agents from the Bundist "Youth Movement."

Accompanied by his 18-year-old secretary, Ludwig made a tour of the East Coast, visiting almost every Army camp and airfield from New York City to Key West, Florida. He prepared reports for the Germans by using a secret ink, code, and an 1834 system of shorthand which he thought no one but the Germans could read—but the FBI solved the riddle.

On June 28, 1941, when the Duquesne spy ring was arrested, Ludwig wrote to his superiors, "I had quite a fright." He was in a store where two of the spies were caught, but arresting Agents pretended not to notice him and allowed him to continue his activities. At the first opportunity, Ludwig cabled Germany: "I missed a serious accident only by inches."

Ludwig fled to a mountain resort in Pennsylvania, and then left alone by automobile for the West Coast. FBI Agents followed close behind. They saw him question soldiers at Selfridge Field in Michigan and change a tire at Wright Field, Ohio, where he could watch activities closely. He was arrested just as he prepared to embark for Japan from the West Coast.

Ludwig made a last desperate attempt to bribe his way to freedom by promising a guard $50,000. The trick failed. He was convicted of espionage and sentenced to twenty years in prison. All other members of his ring were also arrested.

THE PLANNED INVASION OF THE AMERICAS

The Nazi-Fascist teaching of "Divide and Conquer" followed the same pattern in every territory marked for conquest. While Quislings tore down Norway's defenses and the Lavals were hard at work undermining France, the same "softening-up" process was under way in America. The Americas, however, awoke in time and they were the only continents of the world where Axis bombs did not fall or Axis boots did not tread. But the enemy planned it otherwise.

There was never a time in modern history when the entire Western Hemisphere stood in greater danger from foreign invasion than during the critical period of 1941 and 1942. It is only 1,685 miles from Natal, Brazil, to Dakar, North Africa— no further than a railroad trip from Boston, Massachusetts, to Omaha, Nebraska. At one time in those long, anxious months when America was unprepared, German troops were ready at Dakar, waiting the right moment to drive the Nazi knife into Brazil.

The Reich considered a direct attack on American defenses in the Caribbean. German and Japanese planes were to attack the Panama Canal, Colombian seaports and exposed overland pipelines. A fleet of 1,000 huge submarines was to carry Nazi troops into Colombia and Venezuela. A boat was to be sunk in a narrow channel in Suriname—thereby cutting off 60 percent of a mineral necessary to United States industries. Brazil had over 200,000 Japanese. They were reported to be arming. Germans laid plans to smash transportation if Chile broke with the Axis.

The strike in the Bolivian tin mines was traced to a German consul. Slowdowns, fires, and destructive devices slowed the workers on United States bases in Brazil.

The situation had all the elements known in the Axis code of warfare as the preparation for a surprise attack.

"PEARL HARBOR!"

At 1:25 P.M., Sunday, December 7, 1941, the Honolulu office of the FBI called headquarters at Washington, D.C. It was 7:55 A.M. in Hawaii. Japanese bombers were blasting Pearl Harbor!

The first call sparked into action the nation-wide war plans of the FBI. While bombs were still falling on the main United States Pacific fleet, every FBI office from Juneau, Alaska, to San Juan, Puerto Rico, was alerted. Within one hour every FBI employee in each of the field offices was stationed at his post of duty and knew his job. FBI manpower combined with more than 150,000 law enforcement officers to crack down at the slightest sabotage gesture or attempted uprisings of enemy fifth columns.

In the communications center of the FBI, two officials, following FBI war plans worked out in advance, dictated directly to operators the vital messages going out at the same time to all continental field offices over the Bureau's teletype network. Nineteen different messages flashed out in rapid succession and each Special Agent in Charge passed on to cooperating police the latest security orders.

All Japanese known to be dangerous were immediately apprehended. Japanese were taken off planes. Communications in and out of the United States were stopped. Press services to occupied China and Japan were cut off. Protective guards were established at the Japanese, German and Italian Embassies in Washington and at their consulates throughout the country. Their mail and telephone services were discontinued, their funds were frozen.

On the day following Pearl Harbor 1,771 dangerous enemy aliens had been arrested and delivered to the U.S. Immigration and Naturalization Service for detention. As formal declarations of war were announced, large-scale arrests of German and Italian aliens—all known or suspected to be dangerous—were made. The whole operation moved along according to plan. In all, over 16,000 arrests were made by the FBI.

Since the aliens considered "dangerous" were apprehended in a calm and orderly manner, the fears of honest, patriotic aliens were quieted. They saw that there would be none of the so-called "witch hunting" remembered from the last war.

Vicious rumors which flew thick and fast over Hawaii and later spread to the mainland were also quashed by prompt investigations. Official FBI announcements that the "latest stories" were "pure rumor and not real" did much to calm jittery nerves. Public fear was further prevented by a vigorous "Tell it to the FBI" campaign.

Thus, the Axis fifth column was smashed before it could go into action. The panicky fear of it that gripped many Americans in the black days following Pearl Harbor soon disappeared.

EFFECT OF "PEARL HARBOR" IN SOUTH AMERICA

The shock of the Japanese sneak-attack on Pearl Harbor was registered immediately in South American countries. It made them suddenly alert to the prospects of similar attacks.

For more than two years the FBI had found that enemy spying in the United States tied in closely with Axis activities among sister republics to the south. When advised of the information revealed by FBI investigations in the United States, South American countries enthusiastically agreed to cooperate. Many republics asked for FBI liaison agents to work with their own police and intelligence forces. Others sent intelligence officers to train at FBI schools.

The FBI and the law enforcement agencies of the South American countries exchanged information on all matters of mutual interest. In this way an effective Pan-American intelligence force was successfully raised up against the destructive fifth column activities of the Axis spy and sabotage rings in South America.

Altogether, more than 7,000 Axis operators and sympathizers in South America have been expelled or removed far inland where they are harmless. More than 250 spies and saboteurs have been exposed and neutralized. Twenty-nine secret short-wave radio stations used principally to transmit information about the United

States to Germany have been eliminated. Potentially dangerous Axis nationals have been brought under observation.

Such victories have played a major role in the defense of the Western Hemisphere. The massing of German troops at Dakar, the Japanese plans to attack Alaska, to smash through to the West Coast, to bomb the Panama Canal and spread destruction in American war plants—all these were dreams of the enemy. But they failed because the enemies' spy network in the Americas was smashed.

WORLD WAR II BRINGS THE SHOWDOWN

"Pearl Harbor" aroused American spirit to the boiling point and sent the nation's war-production sky-rocketing. But the hour was late. America had the resources, but months were necessary to change the mountains of raw material into enough guns, planes, tanks and ships to defeat the Axis with its seven-year head start. As the race against time began, industrial leaders expressed a universal hope—that there would be no sabotage. Given time, manpower and unmolested machinery, they could do the job. But wartime sabotage in certain key plants producing scarce materials might bottleneck the entire arsenal of Democracy. Plant managers reexamined FBI recommendations for plant security—reflected on the wisdom of the plant survey program begun two years before. But the memory of World War I, when enemy agents blew up American arsenals, railroad yards, ships and factories led some industrialists to wonder. Could sabotage be prevented?

FBI agents remove explosives and equipment buried
on a Florida beach by Nazi saboteurs.

LANDING OF THE EIGHT SABOTEURS

In June 1942, two Nazi U-boats stole into American waters and each landed four German saboteurs on the Eastern coast of the United States. With $174,588 in U.S. bills and enough explosives to last for two years, these saboteurs hastened to New York and Chicago to make plans for their campaign of destruction and terrorism.

Orders from their Nazi superiors had been plain: Dynamite the Hell Gate Bridge in New York. Destroy critically needed aluminum plants. Place time bombs in lockers of railroad stations. Use incendiary pencils. Start fires in large department stores. Spread terror. Make it appear as though an army of saboteurs was at work.

All eight were carefully selected for their jobs. Though born in Germany, each saboteur had spent several years in the United States and knew the country, the customs, and the language. Their instructor at the sabotage school near Berlin had been Walter Kappe, key organizer of the German-American Bund in the old days, who had returned to Germany just before the war. Rated as a "valuable" member of the Nazi Party, Kappe took over the recruiting and training of saboteurs. These eight saboteurs were his first "graduates." Their forged Selective Service and Social Security cards, their technical training, their timing devices for bombs, and their possession of money in large denominations— all these disclosed how important was their mission to the German High Command.

But the mission failed. In less than two weeks after landing, members of the sabotage ring were in FBI custody. Agents trailed them to determine their contacts. But there were no secret armies of the fatherland to welcome them.

By Presidential order they were turned over to a military commission for trial, and on August 8, 1942, six were sentenced to death, one to life imprisonment and one to thirty years.

THE ENEMY WITHIN

In quick succession during this same period, the FBI disclosed operations of numerous other enemy agents.

In New York, a woman doll dealer was arrested for sending information on West Coast naval secrets to the Japanese. A naturalized German-American in Detroit helped speed the flight of an escaped Nazi prisoner and both were caught. In the same city a little group of traitors worked with a "Countess" who had been caught by the FBI shortly after her arrival from Europe. She agreed to work with the FBI and seven from the ring were convicted. A New York "bus boy" tried to hide his identity by using names and addresses of persons selected at random from a telephone directory for return addresses on his secret ink letters. But he was found among New York's millions and was sent to prison.

There were others. They, too, were found by the FBI and felt the hand of American justice.

CRIME ATTEMPTS A COMEBACK

Although busy keeping ahead of world-wide enemy espionage, FBI Agents kept a sharp watch on the forces of the underworld. Just as had been feared, the same murderous, gangster-ridden interests who threatened the security of American life in the crime wave of the '30s promptly took advantage of the first chance to make a comeback.

Considering the nation too busy with the war to bother with criminal activities, these gangsters again proved that few criminals who betray their country in peacetime are changed by the threatened destruction of the nation by war. War simply added to their "opportunities." But this time, as the underworld empire began gathering its forces for action along the home front, it found a situation which its criminal cunning had not foreseen.

American law enforcement was better equipped, better trained, stronger and more determined than ever before in the history of the nation.

In New York, an old-time member of the "Dutch" Schultz Gang led four of his henchmen on a hijacking raid involving $100,000 worth of merchandise. FBI Agents came up as they bound and gagged two truck drivers, before making off with the loot. Stopping the hijackers in their tracks, the Agents released the truck drivers, recovered the merchandise and packed the surprised hoodlums off to be tried and convicted. Their sentences totaled 68 years.

In Pennsylvania and New Jersey, a $450,000 nylon hosiery black market was smashed as several racketeers tried to convert nylon intended for parachutes into nylon for 42,000 pairs of stockings. In Chicago, Roger Touhy, Basil Banghart and members of their gang were captured after escaping from the Illinois State Penitentiary. Two members of the gang, McInerney and O'Connor, tried to shoot it out. Both were killed.

Several thousand fugitives have been captured by the FBI since the outbreak of the war. These have included such dangerous characters as Jacob Drucker, member of "Murder, Inc.;" Irving Carl Chapman, gunman, bank robber and kidnapper who fired on

Special Agents and was killed in the gun battle; Jack K. Meredith, widely known confidence man with more than a hundred different names; Kinnie Wagner, hill-billy gunman and murderer who shot and killed five police officers. A few hours after his arrest, Wagner squinted through the bars of a prison cell at Lynchburg, Virginia, and remarked to a fellow prisoner: "It's a mistake to break a federal law. They will hunt you down for a thousand years."

In his pocket Wagner carried a frayed cartoon. It showed a woman looking through the bars at a convict. She was asking, "Do any of your friends come here to see you?" The convict replied, "No, lady. They're all in here with me."

STRENGTH THROUGH UNITY

During the 1930s and 1940s the FBI has received widespread cooperation and support from police agencies throughout the country. Without it, the work of the FBI would be greatly handicapped. But the FBI has opposed any national police system and has maintained that the answer to effective law enforcement is not nationwide consolidation but scientific training, careful selection of personnel and wholehearted cooperation between agencies in all matters of mutual interest. The real test was proving the accuracy of this law enforcement blueprint.

FBI HEADQUARTERS—WASHINGTON, D.C.

From the FBI Headquarters in Washington, D.C. is supervised the network of 56 field divisions covering the United States and her territorial possessions. Every case investigated in the field is supervised and coordinated at Washington.

Like a highly-geared war plant, the FBI has its assembly lines, its central service pools, and its machinery to bolster the senses of sight and sound so that experts may harness the physical sciences in their war against spies, saboteurs and criminals.

The FBI has been designated by Congress to maintain a

nationwide survey on crime trends in the United States. This national crime barometer permits police throughout the country to keep in touch with the activities of the criminally inclined—to meet them forewarned and forearmed.

Watching the FBI machinery, making certain it functions effectively, is the job of the FBI Director. The morale, discipline, loyalty and efficiency of an organization are no stronger than its chief's.

The vast majority of criminals immediately confess when arrested by the FBI; and, not too strangely, many have complimented the FBI on the fair treatment given them. Law breakers have learned that FBI Agents "get the facts first." When a man is arrested, it is because evidence has been developed pointing to his guilt. During the 1944 fiscal year, 97.28 percent of all criminals investigated by the FBI and prosecuted in Federal Court were convicted.

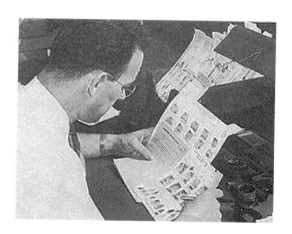

POSITIVE IDENTIFICATION

Among the Bureau's specialized services in Washington is the Integrated Automated Fingerprint Identification System, or IAFIS. IAFIS contains over 250 million sets of fingerprints—the largest collection in the world. Millions of these prints are from the armed services. Every man and woman in the Army, Navy, Marine Corps and Coast Guard is on record with the FBI. Several million fingerprints have also been sent in by civilians for their individual protection and security.

In a section by itself are the fingerprints of lawbreakers: criminal records on more than six million persons—one out of every 22 in the United States. Hundreds of wanted criminals are identified monthly as their fingerprints are checked through the files.

This identification clearing house serves police agencies throughout the country. Incoming records arrive at the rate of 20,000 to 30,000 per day in 1945. More than 70 percent of the prints received from police agencies are identified with previous records. Criminals who a few years ago fled from state to state to escape detection now find themselves identified regardless of where they are arrested. And any police agencies listing a criminal as "wanted" are immediately notified when the fugitive is located. More than a thousand fugitives are identified in this manner each month.

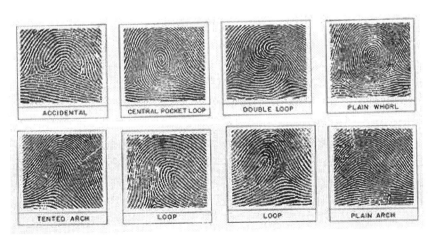

Since fingerprints offer a known means of positive identification, the value of this collection to the American people is beyond calculation. It frequently is responsible for the identification of amnesia and accident victims. Its files contain many touching stories on broken family circles which have been mended through the assistance of fingerprint records.

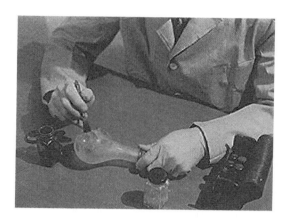

Not long ago the FBI received from a West Coast mother a copy of prints made of her son's fingers when he was three years old. She wrote that family troubles had forced a separation long ago, and she wanted help in locating the child she had not seen for 17 years.

The baby prints were matched quickly with those of a fine young American in the Armed Services. His name had been changed, but the pattern of the fingerprints was the same. A family reunion was made possible.

A soldier bound for overseas duty found his long-missing father within a few hours after turning to the FBI for aid. Another man had gone for years without knowing his real identity because of loss of memory. The FBI filled in the gap from its fingerprint files.

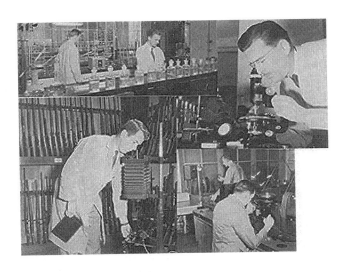

SCIENCE US. CRIME

In 1932 the FBI Laboratory was established to provide scientific aids in criminal investigations. Experts, whose efficiency is judged by the skill of their work and not by the number of convictions in their cases, develop secret writing, identify handwriting, examine firearms, develop latent fingerprints, examine explosives, hairs, fibers, blood stains and conduct thousands of other examinations annually. From small flecks of paint or particles of shattered glass taken in a hit-and-run accident, scientists have been able to tell the make, model or type of car involved. They test the tensile strength of metals; detect inferior quality goods and workmanship in cases of fraud against the Government. They can tell whether a jimmy was used to pry open some lock, whether a certain hammer was used in breaking a safe dial, or whether a pair of pliers cut a piece of wire.

Shortly before the invasion of France the FBI checked on flaws in land-mine detectors and helped correct difficulties in the manufacture of this device.

In a criminal case submitted by local officers, a fragment of cloth on a bullet fired at a burglar was identified as having come from the suspect's clothing. In another investigation, particles of dust and tiny pieces of trash left at the scene of a crime connected a suspect with an aggravated offense. Officers called to investigate a hit-and-run case in the MidWest sent in pieces of broken glass and small chips of automobile paint from the crime scene. These were studied by the FBI experts, who were able to tell the local officers the kind of car which the hit-and-run driver owned. An arrest and conviction followed. A thief who stole automobile tires cut off the numbers by which they could be identified. The FBI experts treated the tires and were able to read the numbers, proving that the tires had been owned by a particular person.

To help them, the FBI scientists in 1945 had the newest laboratory equipment, including microscopes, cameras, optical micrometers and ultraviolet lights. Also for their use are many reference collections such as blood sera, dynamite wrappers, headlight lenses, paper watermarks, typewriter standards, animal hairs, rope samples, automobile paints, heel prints and tire treads.

In this laboratory, the spy, saboteur, murderer, extortionist, bank robber and kidnapper are all trapped by the findings of science. Not only are these facilities used by the FBI in its work but they are also available to local law enforcement agencies without cost.

Since the FBI is a fact-finding agency, its investigations are as important in clearing the innocent as in convicting the guilty. In many instances where circumstantial evidence has pointed to innocent persons, scientific findings of the FBI have cleared them.

In the early 1940s an officer brought to the FBI Laboratory scrapings taken from the fender of a blood-stained automobile and other specimens from a bloody spot on the shoulder of a highway. He said two boys had driven the car but would not explain the presence of the blood. A hit-and-run death was suspected, but no body had been found.

An FBI technician made tests while the officer waited. In a short time he had the answer: the stains were from beef blood. While the boys may have run over a cow, no person had been killed as suspected.

In another case, a soldier was suspected of writing bad checks. An FBI handwriting examination proved the serviceman was not to blame, though circumstances had pointed strongly toward him as the guilty person. The technicians then went one step further. They identified the real author of the bad checks from his handwriting.

TRAINING FOR SERVICE

The FBI's training facilities are maintained in Washington. At the peak of the war expansion program up to 1,000 employees were in training at the same time. At the FBI Academy in nearby Virginia, newly appointed Special Agents received their first training. Here they were given more than 1,000 hours of lecture instruction—the equivalent of two and one-half years of college work. Classes were from nine in the morning until nine at night for four months. Already qualified as lawyers or accountants, they were trained as expert investigators and they qualified as experts in firearms—the Thompson sub-machine gun, the rifle, the shotgun and the pistol. A daily class in athletic training kept them trim. Agents in service return periodically for refresher courses.

So effective has such training been that the FBI National Academy was created in 1955 to give selected police officers from all parts of the country training as police instructors. Returning home, they pass the training on to their fellow officers. Through this program more than 100,000 peace officers have been given expert instruction in the "higher learning" of their profession.

"FIDELITY, BRAVERY, INTEGRITY"

In one of the rooms of the Department of Justice Building hangs the great blue and gold seal of the FBI. Engraved on the crown of the seal are the words: "Fidelity, Bravery, Integrity."

Beneath the seal hangs the bronze memorial plaque bearing the names of the Special Agents who have died in line of duty. Behind that list is a history of battles in the crusade against crime. From it have come the traditions of the FBI.

Connected with one of these names is a page of history which illustrates the ideals of those who serve their country through the Federal Bureau of Investigation.

A Special Agent was mortally wounded in a gun battle with two notorious bank robbers. He lived long enough to identify his murderers, who were caught and executed. After being urged to rest quietly his last words were: "Tell Mr. Hoover I did my best."

"I did my best," became a part of the FBI creed.

The FBI Investigates Hill-billy Killer Kinnie Wagner

It was a cold, frosty morning—an ideal day for Christmas Eve. Kinnie Wagner watched the coffee boiling in the tin pot on the little pot-bellied stove and whistled tunelessly. Snow had fallen during the night covering the ground with a luxurious ermine blanket and the early morning stillness was pregnant with an air of hushed expectancy.

Kinnie Wagner in 1926

ATTEMPTED ARREST ENDS IN MURDER

Kinnie glanced idly out the frosted window. As his eyes wandered across the yard and up the trail, he suddenly started. Four men were approaching on horseback. Quickly he strode across the rough-hewn floor to the door and pulled it open. He watched apprehensively as Sheriff Turner and his three deputies dismounted from their horses.

"What do you want?" Kinnie shouted and his hand stole to his revolver at his side.

"We want you, Wagner, for suspicion of robbery and jail-breaking," Deputy Freeman shouted back.

Kinnie felt himself seized by an overwhelming impulse to run, to break for the open. His horse was across the yard and down the way a spell and with a bit of luck he might make it. Taking his chances, Kinnie bolted from the cabin. His feet encased in high knee boots, stumbled clumsily on the frozen snow.

Deputy Macintosh opened fire with a shotgun. There was a sharp report and the ensuing load hit Kinnie along the belt line, numbing a part of his body and glancing off into the side of the cabin.

Kinnie pulled out his revolver but the shots from the deputy's gun had rendered it useless. He turned in his tracks and dashed wildly back into the cabin; his progress accompanied by the clipped shots from Macintosh.

Slamming the front door, Kinnie threw the bolt. As he leaned panting against the heavy door, he heard them running towards the cabin, shouting, "Give up, Wagner, we've got you cornered." His eyes flitted anxiously around the room and fell on his shotgun. Seizing the weapon, he raised it to his shoulder, took careful aim through the window, and fired both barrels point blank at Macintosh.

The shots found their mark, for the man screamed in anguish as he slumped slowly to the ground. Kinnie waited momentarily to see if he would rise again—his gun ready—but the figure lay motionless. The Sheriff and the others were running over to their fallen comrade. They turned Macintosh over on his back and Kinnie saw the snow stained crimson.

He backed away from the window as the gun slipped from his trembling hands. The three men had straightened up from their inspection of Macintosh and with raised guns and grim faces they closed in on the cabin.

Almost stumbling in his haste, Kinnie wrenched open the rear door to the cabin. As he slipped out into the open, he heard them breaking in the front window and he hastened his steps. But they were close behind him and shots were peppering at his heels as he made for the first clump of scrub pines. Suddenly, he felt a heavy blow on his back and then sharp, swift pain. He doubled over and then desperately clinging to consciousness, dragged his feet over that last stretch. Finally, he reached the little bay mare. She was saddled and waiting. Painfully, he pulled himself up on to the mare's broad back.

"Go, Nellie," he whispered through pain-clenched teeth as he pulled in the reins and feebly clicked his spurs. "I've just killed a man!"

Kinnie Wagner escaped from the authorities that Christmas eve of 1924 with a back full of buckshot and the brand of "killer" freshly engraved on his soul. The taste of drawn blood was new and strange to him for this was his first murder.

He fled to the Appalachians which he called his home, to Clinch Mountain, his front porch. He knew every rock and crag in that section of Virginia, having been born there twenty years ago.

A CIRCUS MARKSMAN ON THE RUN

His guns, still warm from their encounter with the law in Mississippi, were to continue being his impenetrable armor, protecting him from his enemies—the law. For Kinnie Wagner was a "natural" with guns. His skill as a trick-shot artist was already widely known. It dated back to his employment with a circus at seventeen when he had run away from home.

Kinnie had thrilled circus audiences for nearly three years with his amazing feats. He specialized in shooting buttons off a man's vest; tossing walnuts in the air and splintering them with revolver bullets; and lining up cartridges—picking them off—one at a time, without aiming.

As the days in hiding lengthened into weeks, the weeks to months—Kinnie grew restless for the world beyond the mountains. He ventured to Tennessee. It was April 13, 1925, when Kinnie met some of his friends on the banks of the Houston River near Kingsport....

Stretched out on the grassy embankment, Kinnie placed his hands behind his head and watched the clouds tracing lacy patterns in the blue skies. Jed had just made some amusing comment and the girls were laughing heartily.

"Say, it looks like we're gonna have company!" exclaimed Jed as he glanced over the embankment towards the river. "Where?"

"Comin' up the river-path. Looks like the law!"

Kinnie sat up abruptly and stared down the path. Swallowing hard, he whispered softly, "Keep on talkin' as if nothin's happened. I'll sneak down the side here and swim 'cross. They'll never see me."

As he rose to his feet, his hands fingered his guns and he whispered, "So long, gals."

THREE MURDERS IN MISSISSIPPI

Kinnie made his way cautiously through the brush. A few more yards now and he'd hit the path with the river just beyond. Suddenly, the air resounded with the sharp spat-spat of bullets. Kinnie wheeled around—his guns automatically cradled in his large hands. His eyes searched the path and quickly found their target half-hidden in a clump of bushes. He aimed the brass buttons on the blue-coated figure and fired in rapid bursts until the man fell backwards into the marsh.

Kinnie dashed behind an old Sycamore tree as a second volley of shots sprayed the path around him and thudded dully into the thick bark. From a silver-mounted cartridge belt he reloaded his smoking guns. Cautiously stepping into the open again, Kinnie gazed intently among the moss-hung foliage. Suddenly he caught sight of a second blue-coated figure moving up along the marsh. The officer saw Kinnie at almost the same instant. Both men raised their guns and several shots rang out. The officer crumpled slowly to the ground with an incredulous expression on his face and an un-fired gun, still clenched in his hand.

There was a sudden hushed silence broken only by the sighing of the wind as it filtered through the marsh grass. Kinnie felt his blood pounding in his veins. His instinct told him he was cornered in the river bottom. Crouching low, he stole across the path and into the marsh. Dank reeds licked his boots with moist tongues and clung possessively to his legs as he made for the protective shelter of an overhanging ledge of the embankment. Suddenly, he started and held his breath. Something was moving on the embankment. Kinnie dropped silently to his knees and quickly checked his guns. Still crouched low and almost concealed by the tall grass, he stealthily edged forward until he was close enough to see more clearly. A man with a sheriff's star pinned prominently to his chest was leaning over the ledge, gun in hand. Kinnie made a slight movement. As the unsuspecting officer whirled and started in his direction, Kinnie's bullet lodged in his heart. The body toppled over the edge of the embankment and fell onto the path.

With one thought burning in his mind—to get away—to flee—Kinnie hastily scrambled up the side of the embankment and crawled through the thick brush. The girls were just where he had left them only both were sobbing hysterically. Jed was talking to them.

Kinnie moved up quietly. His voice was flat, expressionless, as he addressed Jed. "Give me that horse."

Jed turned. His face whitened as he saw Kinnie.

"But you killed 'em, Kinnie. We saw you...." His voice died to a whisper as Kinnie impatiently fingered his revolver.

"I mean no foolishness with you, Jed. I want that horse!"

Jed stepped back reluctantly as Kinnie jumped into the saddle.

He picked up the reins and galloped off up the river and on through the underpass.

Kinnie Wagner's bullets killed two men that day—Deputy Sheriff Hubert Webb and Policeman John Smith. One shot penetrated Webb's face just left of his nose while another grazed his shoulder and passed through his heart. Either wound would have proven almost instantly fatal. Smith was shot directly through his heart. The third man, Officer Frazier, was shot through the left breast, the bullet coming out through the left shoulder. Although it was not believed by the attending physicians at that time to be fatal, Frazier died a number of years later due to the wound.

By five o'clock of the same afternoon a posse of officers and deputized citizens had been organized and were in hot pursuit of the fugitive. The whole countryside, notified by telephone and telegraph, was aroused as the roads, fields and woodlands were scoured in every direction. Bloodhounds took up the trail where the horse had been found exhausted, but to no avail. Kinnie Wagner was as elusive as he was deadly and the posse returned empty-handed.

REFUGE WITH A WIDOW

Meanwhile shortly before midnight, Kinnie, nearly exhausted, came to the home of Mrs. W. S. Rhodes, a widow near Waycross, Virginia, and talked to her through the window. He told her at that time he wanted to get a pencil and some paper, as he wished to write a note to his people, declaring that he was going to kill himself.

His note read: "Dear Sister: Believe they will get me, so I will fix things so you will go through school."

As Kinnie stood in the darkness talking to Mrs. Rhodes, he tried to keep the growing panic from mounting up into his voice but the words still spilled out breathlessly, "Lady, I've done some dirt. They're looking for me...." His voice faded off.

"Who are you?"

"Kinnie Wagner, Madam."

The woman patted his shoulder gently and she said, "Wait just a minute. I'm going to put you up in the barn for the night."

She pulled the window down softly, threw a light shawl over her shoulders, and picked up a kerosene lamp. As she came to the door, she turned the wick low and whispered, "Come along, young fellow. You'll feel better after you've rested in the hayloft for a few hours."

Kinnie followed the woman across the yard and into the barn. His clothes were damp and his body shook with chills for he had swum across Possum Creek that night in his mad dash for freedom. He tried to find words to express his gratitude. The woman shook her head and picked up the lantern to leave.

"Trust in the Lord, Kinnie Wagner. Rest a while. I'll be back later."

She closed the barn door quietly after her. Kinnie threw himself down on the fragrant hay and buried his weary head in his arms. The darkness was comforting but he knew daylight would come only too soon.

KINNIE SURRENDERS

Early the next morning, kindly old Mrs. Rhodes returned to the barn to talk to Kinnie. She advised him to surrender and "save his soul." Although Kinnie wasn't used to having women change his mind, Widow Rhodes convinced him. Consequently, on the same morning, April 14, 1925, Kinnie Wagner quietly gave himself up to D. R. Poe at the latter's store near Waycross, Virginia.

On surrendering to the storekeeper, Kinnie remarked he had killed as many as he wanted and was now ready to surrender without any further violence. However, he said he was not willing to give up to an officer of the law, and under no circumstances would he submit to arrest by an officer of the law; he would shoot it out with any number. Kinnie was then placed in the Blountville, Tennessee jail.

The machinery of justice moved with unusual speed for the back country of Tennessee. On April 21, 1925, Kinnie Wagner stood on trial for his life. There were three indictments, two for murder and one for felonious assault. Four days later the jury brought in its verdict, pronouncing Wagner, "guilty."

Kinnie Wagner (right)—Probably taken in 1925 when he was lodged in Blountville Jail.

"DEATH BY ELECTROCUTION!"

As Kinnie stood before the judge to hear the imposition of sentence, the flat nasal tones of the spokesman responded through the court room. "Death by electrocution!"

Guards led Kinnie away to his cell in the county jail and mountain people in a dozen counties breathed a sigh of relief when they heard the news. Forces of law and order had triumphed and justice had received its due. But little did they suspect what was brewing in the mind of Kinnie Wagner as he sat moodily in his cell awaiting his fate.

The heat of a late afternoon July sun poured in slanting rays on the roadway and made the dusty clothes of the prisoners cling damply to their shoulders.

The road gang marched wearily, the mark of prison in their hopeless faces and shoulders. Little puffs of dust spiraled and vanished as they plodded along under the shotguns of the two guards.

They were tired—but they were lucky. A long day of hard work under a hot sun was tough, but not nearly as tough as sitting all day in a barred cell thinking the thought that must be running through Kinnie's mind—"Death by electrocution!"

Did he mark the days—the hours? Did he feel the minutes slipping by and find himself counting the monotonous ticking of his watch as it checked off the moments of his life?

They were at the door and the jailor swung it back. The road gang entered noisily. They were hungry and in their thought of food they forgot Kinnie Wagner's troubles. He had killed three men and wounded another and he'd been sentenced to burn for it. That was his lookout. They were the lucky ones.

The jailor looked at his watch. It was six o'clock.

"Come along, boys."

Two of the prisoners followed. The guards were close behind, each armed with a .38 automatic. It was a daily chore, putting these two into the prisoner's cage. The jailor was at the head of the stairway, keys rattling on the ring in his hand.

A chorus of voices greeted him. He answered cheerfully.

"Evening boys. Hungry? How are you, Kinnie?"

He turned the key in the lock, the cell door opened, and the evening quiet of the jail was ripped with a torrent of sound and action.

JAIL BREAK!

Men erupted from the cage. A bottle crashed down on the jailor's head and he wilted into unconsciousness, his mouth still open. Kinnie Wagner pounced on him, groping for his gun. Prisoners flung themselves on the startled guards, seized their automatics before their surprise-numbed muscles could react.

"Come on! Move!"

Kinnie Wagner was in charge. He marshalled the mad rush down the stairs. Two men hurried out of the rear door; another scrambled through the kitchen window. A helper at the jail on the outside saw one of the prisoners dash through the front door; he lifted his gun and a woman inmate stepped in the way. He held his fire—and Kinnie Wagner's big form broke from the door, running. Wagner snapped a quick shot at the prison helper, missed him and dashed down the road in the wake of another escapee.

The pair crossed a small field, ducked into a woodlot and disappeared. The other five melted into the dusky shadows of Reedy Creek.

The uproar at the jail roused the village. The screams of hysterical women inmates and excited shouting of guards mixed with the noise of running feet and confused questioning.

Citizens were deputized; posses formed. Hundreds of armed officers combed three Tennessee counties.

But Kinnie Wagner was gone. It was as if the fugitive had merged with the trees and the dark mountains. There was no trail; not the faintest hint that a fugitive murderer had passed.

Much later Wagner was to tell of a hurried flight to Mexico; of fleeing through the fingers of the law and swimming the Rio Grande to Chihuahua south of the border. He told of a week in Mexico; of trying to find the location of a railroad by asking its whereabouts in sign language of a Mexican boy who warned him to stay clear of a revolution that was in progress.

SETTLING DOWN IN TEXARKANA, ARKANSAS

Returning to the United States, Kinnie Wagner travelled continuously until the chase had cooled somewhat. He liked the country and mountain people. Twenty-five miles from Texarkana, Arkansas, he settled down. He found work in a saw mill and roomed with Sam Carper, who, with his brothers Bob and William, enjoyed a notorious and unsavory reputation. Two of the brothers were out on bail at the time for picking a fight with a sixteen-year-old boy.

Kinnie Wagner was to play a grim and deadly part in the lives of the Carper brothers.

Bob and William and Kinnie spent a lazy afternoon. Kinnie didn't like Bob Carper. He sat on a log bench, feet braced against a twisted length of pine wood. Long curls of thin white wood spiraled from the splinter he was whittling.

Bob Carper came to the door wiping his mouth with the back of his hand. The odor of whiskey hung heavily about him. He slouched against the door jamb and grinned insolently at Kinnie Wagner.

Wagner's eyes were cold, his voice expressionless.

"Goin' kinda heavy on that likker, Bob. Better lay off 'til it's split even."

"Gittin' kinda high-handed, ain't you, Kinnie?"

"You name it. I want my fair cut."

"Fair's fair. I'll split it even."

"I don't trust you're even."

They were quarreling suddenly, like a pair of stubborn children. Bob Carper lurched to the table, seized a fruit jar half full of the pale yellow liquor and flung it through the open window.

Kinnie Wagner's eyes were hostile and ugly. His hand flicked to a gun and slowly withdrew.

"Bob, I could 'a shot you like a yellow-bellied rattler. Come on out here and let's settle this fair—with guns."

William Carper intervened quickly. "He's drunk, Wagner. You leave him be 'till he's sober. You-all started this."

Sam Carper rode up as the quarrel blazed hotly.

"Bob, you leave Kinnie be. Ain't no call to be pickin' on him."

There was a lull while Sam Carper drank deeply of the fiery liquor.

They were at the crude little enclosure where the Carpers kept their horses when the argument flared up again.

KINNIE KILLS AGAIN

Kinnie Wagner's hot temper was out of bounds and Sam had drunk enough to join the quarrel.

"See here, Wagner, you can't say that about my kinfolk! Get him, Bob!"

Kinnie Wagner had shot the buttons off of coats as a circus stunt and the bullet from his gun went through Sam Carper with clean finality. He fired a second shot as one of the Carpers hurled a single-tree with stunning force against his jaw. The gun thundered a third time and was still.

Lillie Barker, the woman sheriff of Texarkana, Arkansas, opened the door of her office on August 18, 1926, to find a powerfully built giant offering her his guns.

There must have been an incongruous streak of vanity, twisted chivalry and a superb sense of showmanship blended in Kinnie Wagner's warped mind.

"I come to surrender, ma'am. I jist shot two men."

Wagner towered over the startled little sheriff.

"What are you talking about?"

"Two Gun" Kinnie pressed the guns into Lillie Barker's limp hands.

"You're bounden to hear it sooner or later. Like as not you know the Carpers ... Sam and William...."

"Well?"

"I killed 'em, ma'am. Shot 'em. Got Bob, too, but he ain't dead. He's still kickin' like a trussed up fowl...."

The sheriff stared unbelievingly. Kinnie Wagner watched for some sign of recognition. There was none.

"My name's Harvey Logan, ma'am. I ... "

Lillie Barker motioned to her lanky deputy.

"Search him, Jack. Use that empty cell. I'm goin' to check up on this...."

Kinnie grinned as she went out. If he could just sit tight without being recognized until this blew over....

Lillie Barker returned at dusk. She was accompanied by grim-looking men carrying cocked rifles. She strode indignantly to the bars of Kinnie's cell.

"'Harvey Logan,' indeed! You're Kinnie Wagner and you're wanted in four states for murder!"

Kinnie's eyes blazed for a moment; then he laughed.

"Well, ma'am, they killed the Lord for being too good and they're gonna kill me, I guess, for bein' too bad, so you see, you lose at either end of the road."

BACK TO MISSISSIPPI

Arkansas gave Kinnie Wagner to Mississippi to stand trial for the Christmas Eve murder of Deputy Murdock Macintosh in 1924.

He was sentenced to life imprisonment after a three-day trial and the Travelling Sergeant of the Mississippi State Penitentiary at Parchman came to Meridian to take Kinnie Wagner back.

As the train neared Jackson, the five-time killer shifted his muscular long body in the seat. He appeared to be dozing.

The sergeant from the penitentiary eyed him closely, hand on his gun. The train was slowing almost to a stop. Kinnie Wagner stirred again. He twisted restlessly; then with a sudden sharp lunge was upright, striving to break away.

The fist of the stocky warden flashed out and up. It caught the killer flush on the point of his jaw and cracked sharply against the bone. Kinnie Wagner's head snapped back, his eyes glazed, and the body of the big mountaineer slumped slowly down. He was out cold.

So "Two-Gun" Kinnie began his course at the "University," as he called Mississippi State Penitentiary. But steel and brick and man-made walls did not hold Kinnie Wagner.

AT "THE UNIVERSITY"

The guard wasn't a small man but standing next to Kinnie Wagner he appeared undersized and dwarfed. Kinnie's huge frame towered over as the guard spoke excitedly.

"Here's a gun, Wagner. One of the prisoners has escaped and you're to be in the posse. Warden says it's okay."

"Right with you, Mac. Wanna use my dogs as well as the bloodhounds?"

The guard nodded his head affirmatively and hurried away—his steps echoing faintly through the cement hall.

Kinnie Wagner breathed exultingly as he slipped on a loose jacket over his penitentiary suit. It had been quite a while since one of the boys had flown the coop and he was raring for the excitement of the chase.

As he walked swiftly down the hall, he chuckled at the changes time had wrought. Who would have ever thought that "Two Gun" Kinnie would ever be a trustee—guarding other prisoners and recapturing escapees? He—a five-time killer and lifer. That "good behavior" was paying dividends.

The jail door shut noisily after him as he stepped out into the prison yard. From a thick leather leash held easily in his right hand, a pack of bloodhounds and his two police dogs, strained—pawing the loose earth and vying among themselves for the shrillest yelps. Their enthusiastic baying cut the silence as he deliberately paused to check the gun. It was a .38 caliber repeating Winchester. He ran his free hand over the smooth, steel surface almost lovingly before tucking it under his arm.

The rest of the posse were still pouring out of the building, strapping on their guns, as Kinnie, loosening his grip on the leash slightly, permitted himself to be turned in the direction the dogs were pulling—to the west. It was after six. The dying rays of the sun were flooding the sky with streamers of crimson and violet, bathing the distant green hills in a golden haze.

As Kinnie gazed on them momentarily, he felt an overwhelming nostalgia sweep over him for those hills and mountains he called home—the Appalachians—and for the mountain folk he had known so intimately as a boy.

It had been many years since he had roamed the Virginia hillsides with the braggadocio of a mountain lion and the cunning of a red fox. He was thirty-seven now—no longer the impetuous youth with a quick trigger finger who killed men easily with reckless abandon. Fourteen long years in the "University," as he humorously referred to the Penitentiary, were behind him. After an unsuccessful attempt to escape in 1927, he had spent those years in winning the confidence of the prison authorities. He had hoed cotton wearily day after day, month after month, in the stifling summer heat. During the dreary winter months he had trained a pair of shepherd police dogs and had given little performances with them for his fellow prisoners as well as using them to track down escapees.

A TRUSTED TRUSTY ESCAPES

There had been plenty of time to think—plenty of time to plan his next move. And as Kinnie turned slowly back to join the assembled posse, his pulse beat rapidly. He knew that this was to be the night. He was going to make a break himself. He could resist the urge to be free no longer.

There were ten men in the posse, each trusty assigned as companion to a guard. Kinnie's hope soared high when he found himself paired with Mac.

"Now, stick close to me, Wagner. We gotta keep together with the rest of the men," Mac warned as Kinnie and the dogs piled into the open car.

Kinnie grunted affirmatively as Mac stepped on the starter. They were the last car in the group. "How far we ridin', Mac?" Kinnie queried as the long line of cars began to move.

"Down to the river bank 'bout ten miles. Then you and the dogs'll take over."

Kinnie smiled silently in agreement. Yes, he planned to take over, but not in the manner Mac expected. He ran his hand over his square jaw and stared steadily ahead.

The distance between the cars widened as they raced along the shadowy highway. Mac, a slow, cautious driver, was rapidly falling back in the procession.

"It's gonna be so dark in a few minutes that we'll never find that bird," Mac grunted as he gingerly stepped the car up a bit.

Kinnie nodded and cast a speculative eye at the swiftly darkening sky. The dogs in the back seat, as if aware of the approaching night, were howling in unison above the wind.

"Can't trust one of them prisoners worth a darn. Make 'em a trusty and what'a they do when your back's turned? Run away."

Mac grumbled on and then, noting Kinnie's silence, magnanimously offered, "All except you, Wagner. I sed to myself when I saw the warden made you a trusty. Now there's a man kin be trusted."

He turned his head slightly to see Kinnie's reaction to the compliment. The huge man, seemingly entirely oblivious to his words, was lying back on the seat—eyes closed, breathing deeply.

"Ain't asleep, are ya, Wagner," Mac persisted. "I need ya to watch the road for me. So dark now I can't see a foot beyond my hand."

Kinnie opened his eyes slowly. The car ahead of them was now barely visible—just two pinpoints of light. It swept around a curve and disappeared from view.

"You're right, Mac, never trust a human bein'. I know from experience. The more I see of dogs, the less faith I have in man."

As Kinnie continued on philosophically, his hand stole stealthily to the gun at Mac's side. He leaned against him heavily as the car turned the curve and slipped the weapon out of the guard's belt.

"Watch those curves, Mac. You're gettin' reckless these days. Almost knocked me over on you."

Kinnie waited breathlessly to see if Mac had felt him remove his gun but the guard drove steadily on; his forehead furrowed as he stared ahead into the night.

"Say, do you see that car that was ahead of us, Wagner? There's a fork along here somewhere I don't wanna miss—goes down by the river."

Kinnie sat tensely. This was the opportunity he'd been waiting for. His eyes narrowed as he watched for the fork. If Mac saw it, he'd have to use the gun. If he didn't, so much the better. This highway they were on led to Clarksdale where he could hide out for awhile before headin' for home.

He held his breath as they approached the fork. Clearing his throat, he tried to speak casually.

"Betta step on it, Mac. Fork's up quite a ways yet. I'll let you know when we come to it."

Kinnie let out a deep sigh and relaxed as Mac stepped on the gas nervously and the car shot by the fork. They tore along the highway for several miles before Mac sensed something amiss.

"Are ya sure, Wagner, we haven't missed it? I never rode this far before."

He turned his head and stared at Kinnie perplexedly.

Kinnie laughed and slipping his gun from his belt, pointed its deadly snout at Mac.

"Betta stop worryin' 'bout the fork, Mac. I've got other plans."

As Mac reached for his gun and stepped on the brake, Kinnie

shoved the weapon in his side.

"I wouldn't try anything, Mac. I've waited fourteen years for this night and nothin's goin' to stop me. Understand?"

The guard shook his head quickly in affirmation and the car picked up speed again and spun along the highway at a rapid clip.

"You're crazy, Wagner, ya know you'll never get away with it."

Kinnie smiled coldly.

"I may not get away with it, as you say, Mac. But, remember, this time I've nothin' to lose by tryin' and a heck of a lot to gain."

His words rang with a deadly finality that cautioned no further comment.

ON THE RUN AGAIN

Kinnie Wagner made good his third prison escape on the night of October 27, 1940. After forcing the guard to drive him to Clarksdale, about forty miles away, he exchanged his prison clothes for the guard's civilian suit, took his money and drove off into the night—a middle-aged man, embittered against the law and armed with a .38 caliber repeating Winchester and a .90 caliber revolver.

For a year while Mississippi authorities searched for the elusive killer, Kinnie Wagner enjoyed the fruits of his liberty operating a profitable liquor store on the Mississippi-Alabama state line.

One of Kinnie Wagner's hideouts, Morrison City, Virginia.

THE FBI BECOMES INVOLVED

In October, 1941, confident that he had successfully eluded the authorities, Kinnie Wagner headed back to southwest Virginia, the mountain country. It was not until June 6, 1942, when a criminal affidavit was sworn out at Sunflower County, Mississippi, charging him with kidnapping the Mississippi State Penitentiary guard that the possibility of the Federal Bureau of Investigation entering the case seemed probable. The resultant complaint, filed before the United States Commissioner at Clarksdale on July 23, 1942, charging Kinnie Wagner with unlawful flight to avoid prosecution for kidnapping and the issuance of a warrant for his arrest, were the beginning of one of the most dangerous and comprehensive man hunts ever recorded in FBI annals.

A dragnet was thrown over Tennessee, Mississippi and neighboring states. Wanted notices were posted: "KINNIE WAGNER WITH ALIASES ... BORN—1903 ... HEIGHT 6'2" ... WEIGHT 220-260 LBS ... EYES BROWN ... HAIR—BLACK, WAVY, SLIGHTLY BALD ... BUILD—ATHLETIC, STANDS VERY ERECT. OCCUPATION—TRICK-SHOT CIRCUS PERFORMER, LABORER ... SCARS—CUT SCAB UNDER CHIN, IRREGULAR CUT SCAR ON BALL OF EACH THUMB ... PECULIARITIES— HEAVY EYEBROWS, LONG FACE ... ESCAPED FROM MISSISSIPPI STATE PENITENTIARY ON OCTOBER 27, 1940."

Deliberately and painstakingly, Special Agents of the FBI fitted the shreds of evidence together. One investigation led to many sections of the country but persistent clues indicated that Kinnie Wagner was hiding out near his birthplace of Gate City, Virginia, a mountainous town located in the Moccasin Gap of the Appalachians.

Every lead developed foretold the deadliness of the hill-billy killer. "Kinnie Wagner is armed with a sawed-off 20-gauge shotgun, two .22 automatic rifles, four revolvers and a load of ammunition. He has reloaded his shotgun shells with ball bearings."

Reports poured in from the terrified mountain folk. "Kinnie Wagner is boasting that if he were shot between the eyes he could hold his breath long enough to kill the man who shot him."

The FBI carried on its man hunt for the hill-billy killer

relentlessly over a period of nine months. As the trail grew warmer, many tips were received as to Kinnie's location. Each lead was carefully investigated but the fugitive seemed to be one step ahead of the law each time.

THE MOVING TARGET—HEAVILY ARMED

Meanwhile, Kinnie, aware that the FBI was looking for him, kept constantly changing his hiding place—moving about in an area about ten miles square between Kingsport, Tennessee, and Gate City, Virginia. He would spend the night in vacant houses, be gone in the morning, and turn up uninvited for meals and lodging at some relative's home in the evening.

It was during these last few months before his capture that Kinnie, in order to keep his trigger finger in practice, would shoot rabbits on the run with his pistols and split wasps in two—those careless enough to light on tree trunks near him.

When meeting friends, he would arrange a designated meeting place; approach the spot with a sawed-off shotgun tucked under one arm and a pint in his hip pocket; and converse sociably for several minutes. After the social visit was over, Kinnie would leave alone—still lugging his gun—and walk along the railroad tracks to wherever he was spending the night. The high elevation of the tracks afforded him an opportunity to see anyone approaching from front or behind.

On one occasion when Kinnie dropped in to see some friends he had known as a boy, he was wearing five guns—two .38 revolvers, one pistol resembling a German Luger, a smaller caliber revolver, one sawed-off shotgun and a full cartridge belt.

LOOKING FOR LIQUOR . . .

It was in the early morning hours of April 16, 1943, a little after 1 A.M. A speeding car, zooming down the Daniel Boone trail in the Moccasin Gap section of Scott County, Virginia, on the road to Gate City drew the attention of an alert FBI Agent. A car driven by a sergeant of the Virginia State Police, and containing three FBI Agents took up the pursuit....

Kinnie Wagner rested his head against the plush seat of the car and watched the surrounding countryside fly by. The moon was shining so brightly that he could distinguish clearly the many familiar landmarks which led to Gate City. It was the driver who spoke first. "Almost there, Smith. Tired?"

Kinnie turned his eyes away from the countryside.

"You oughta know me betta than that, Jack. I'm still rarin' to go, though, guess most of the places'll be closed this time of night in town." Jack chuckled.

"You and the man in the moon oughta get together. You both sleep by day and prowl by night. Can't see how ya do it."

Kinnie stalled in agreement and, as he spoke, he patted the sawed-off shotgun cradled in his arms.

"I and this baby find it mighty convenient to do our callin' at night. I jest ain't sociable in broad daylight. Too many strangers around."

The clock said 1:30 as they drove slowly into town. Most of the homes were completely darkened except for occasional night lights flickering on front porches.

Kinnie yawned and sat up straight. His piercing brown eyes studied the passing homes carefully.

"Wanna keep on Smith? There's a roadhouse outside of town a ways...."

"Well, now you're talkin', bub. Let's go. I feel like jest one more drink 'fore we close up." Kinnie moistened his lips expectantly.

The car picked up speed on the outskirts of town and resumed its course along the Daniel Boone trail—weaving easily along the mountainous terrain.

The car in which Kinnie Wagner was riding when overtaken near Gate City, Virginia. The arrows point to bullet holes made when Wagner dived into a roadside ditch to avoid apprehension.

A HIGH-SPEED CHASE ...

"Smith, did you notice a car followin' us right 'fore we reached town?"

Kinnie snapped his head back sharply and peered for several seconds through the rear window.

"Yes, I did. Nothing to worry 'bout though. It had only one headlight. This 'uns got two."

Kinnie kept his gaze fastened on the trailing car. It followed closely behind them. He tried to discern its occupants but it was useless. As he turned back to Jack, there was a note of apprehension in his voice. "Recognize the car, Jack?"

"Nope."

Kinnie shot another startled glance out the rear window. The car was creeping up steadily, shortening the distance between them. A sudden wave of cold sweat broke out in moist beads on his forehead, and left his hands cold and clammy. He nudged Jack in the side with the shotgun.

"Gotta keep your feet on the gas, Jack, and make this buggy roll. I don't think I'm gonna like it if that car catches up with us. You might get hurt, too."

Jack stole a swift look at Kinnie and the smile froze on his face. "Quit kiddin', Smith. You've got the jitters."

The car swerved slightly as Jack tried to shove the gun away from his side with one arm but Kinnie dug it in even more persistently.

Suddenly, the screaming siren of the rear automobile split the silence of the night. It rose to a shrill crescendo as it pulled closer and closer. Kinnie tried to peer through the rear window but the glaring headlights of the trailing car blinded him. He nudged Jack again with the gun.

"Stop the car! I'm gonna take 'em off guard and then make a break for it! They'll never get me!"

Jack stepped on the brakes and the car screeched to a halt. Men poured out of the trailing car which pulled up about fifty yards behind them.

A voice shouted.

"We're Special Agents of the FBI. Come out of that car with your hands up!"

Trembling, Jack opened the car door and slid out from under the wheel. With hands pointing to the sky, he edged slowly out. Kinnie, however, sat motionless. Only the grim expression on his face indicated that he had heard the command.

It came again ... closer this time ... imperatively.

"We're the FBI. Come out with your hands up."

The fugitive remained frozen in the car.

The command was repeated again.

There was another moment of silence and then Kinnie began to move. Hands up, his gigantic body in a crouched position, he backed out of the car on the side opposite the driver's seat.

As he reached the side of the highway, he made a sudden break for the front of the car which was met with a burst of Thompson submachine gun tracer bullets. Instantly, he dived into a ditch at the side of the highway.

Special Agents immediately threw a spotlight on the ditch. They waited patiently, cautiously.

. . . AND CAPTURE!

Kinnie Wagner crouched in the ditch several minutes before he acknowledged his capture and walked up the embankment reaching skyward. Midway between the two cars, Agents called. "Take off your coat, Wagner."

Kinnie stripped the coat off. Agents could see two .38 revolvers on his left and right sides, carried on a full ammunition belt.

On the command to take off the guns, he stooped to the pavement and dropped them.

A few seconds later the notorious killer of five men who had boasted that if he had his gun on a man, no matter whether he had his hands up or down, he would shoot him, was securely hand-cuffed. The legend of "Two Gun" Kinnie was drawing to a conclusion.

Kinnie Wagner's guns. He was carrying two pistols and a sawed-off shotgun when captured. The rest were secured from his hideout.

When the car in which Kinnie Wagner was riding was searched after his capture, Agents found two additional revolvers and a sawed-off automatic 20-gauge shotgun loaded with five cartridges containing ball bearings instead of buckshot. A vast arsenal uncovered in one of his hideouts included three .38 caliber revolvers;

one .22 caliber pistol; two .22 caliber rifles; one 38-40 rifle; two 20-gauge shotguns; over 1,500 rounds of ammunition; two gun belts; two holsters; and an old canvas rifle bag. He also carried a pair of powerful binoculars and a five-cell flashlight.

The driver of the car who was arrested with Kinnie Wagner told FBI Agents that he first met the fugitive about February 25, 1943, on Pine Ridge of Clinch Mountain in the Appalachian Range. "He introduced himself to me as Joe Smith," recounted the speaker. "He had a sawed-off shotgun in his hands. Wagner told me there were two kinds of people who carried that type of gun—the law and the outlaw. He then told me that he was not the law."

When the news of Kinnie Wagner's capture reached the mountain folk, they were both relieved and saddened. Kinnie Wagner had been to them, while at liberty, a hill-billy John Dillinger. But behind bars, he assumed for them the romantic characteristics of Robin Hood. Accordingly, an overwhelming number of "relatives," allegedly wives, brothers, sisters, cousins and others stormed the Bristol, Virginia, jail, where he was being held, desiring to see "Two Gun" Kinnie.

When Agents questioned Kinnie Wagner concerning his life as a recluse since 1940, he remarked with a guffaw, "I have never been lonesome because I like my own company too well, and as for hobbies, what I like best is to be by myself and think."

On the whole Wagner was extremely loquacious. He would recite poetry and verses to any audience he could obtain.

In spite of the fact that several "wives" had contacted police headquarters at Bristol, he declared that he had never been married. "They locked me up too soon and didn't give me a chance to do any courting."

THE PHILOSOPHER-OUTLAW

The affable outlaw talked frequently to Agents after he was removed to the jail in Lynchburg, Virginia. On one occasion he stated that from the day a human being draws his first breath, he fights a losing battle. He claimed that Methuselah, who lived a thousand years, came nearer to winning the battle of life than anyone whom he had ever heard of and that in the end he lost, also. He pointed out that as much as anyone could hope to achieve in this life would be to lead such a life that it would be an example for other people to follow and thus better civilization. In this regard, he stated, "What a record I'll leave behind me."

When asked at any time how he was getting along, he would state, "I am getting along all right considering; but like the oppressed people of Europe, there's a heck of a lot to be considered."

The Special Agent in Charge of the Richmond Office received a letter from Kinnie Wagner, dated May 1, 1943, written while he was in the Lynchburg Jail. In it he stated:

"I wanted to have a talk with you in earnest before I went south.... If I ever by chance get free regardless of how long I'll come see you if I have to ride an ox to Oregon. If everybody—I mean law—had been as nice as your branch of the service I can truthfully say I would not be in this trouble and after I got in if they had went by facts I'd been freed.... I won't pat your back and then stab it. That's more than some of the so called good can say and if I didn't like a fellow I wouldn't pretend to it if it was Adolph, Tojo or whoever he might be.... I guess I'll catch H—— when I get back. I can't tell what my fate or fortune may be but we none know that. Whatever it is I'll do the best I can with what I have. I know you boys think all folks like me as bad. I wish every American had witnessed everything I have. Was you ever starved, beaten year in and year out by people that been in prison instead of free not because they had a job even or based on merits but obtained through petty political sources? I hope someday your branch of service will have power to check on institutions and see that a prisoner is treated according to law requirements for the benefit of the whole nation...."

On April 17, 1943, Kinnie Wagner waived preliminary hearing before the United States Commissioner at Bristol, Virginia, and was ordered by the United States Commissioner to be held without bail. Wagner amusingly stated afterwards that he didn't want to deal with small shots anyway; he would rather tell his story only to the big shots.

Early in May, 1943, he was removed from the Lynchburg, Virginia, jail and returned to the Mississippi State Penitentiary, Parchman, Mississippi, to continue serving his sentence of life imprisonment.

In December of 1944 Kinnie Wagner sent a postcard to the Richmond Office wishing all a Merry Christmas.

Although "Two Gun" Kinnie no longer haunts the Appalachians of southern Virginia, the memory of his smoking guns and gigantic figure is perpetuated in the hearts of the mountain people as they sing the ballads based on his adventures, This is perhaps the most complete version of his hair-trigger adventures that has been put to verse.

Kinnie Wagner in custody.

"KINNIE WAGNER'S SURRENDER"

I'm sure you've heard my story, From the Kinnie Wagner song:

"How down in Mississippi, I took the road that's wrong.
It was down in Mississippi, Where I murdered my first man
The Sheriff there at Leakesville, For justice took his stand.
Then I went from Mississippi, To the State of Tennessee

Two men went down before me, And they took my liberty.
I wandered through the country, But I never could find rest
'Till I went to Texarkana, Away out in the west.
Again I started drinking, And again I pulled my gun
And within a single moment, The deadly work was done.
The sheriff was a woman, But she got the drop on me
I quit the game and surrendered, Gave up my liberty.
I'm down in Mississippi, And soon shall know my fate
I'm waiting for my trial, But I do not dread my fate
For still the sun is shining, And the sky is blue and fair
But my heart is not repining, For I do not give a care.
I have had my worldly pleasure, I have paid for many a man
But 'twas out in Texarkana, That a woman called my hand.
Young men, young men take warning, And take my last advice
If you start the game in life wrong, You will surely pay the price."

(Words and music by Andrew Jenkins, arranged by Irene Spain, Copyright
September 27, 1926; publisher listed as Polk C. Brockman, Atlanta.)

The Lindbergh Kidnapping

Although the kidnapping and murder of Charles A. Lindbergh, Jr., occurred many years ago, the world still remembers the tragedy vividly. Few people remember, however, the specific facts in the case as they unraveled during the two years following the kidnapping. Many people, in fact, wonder if the case was ever completely solved. Was the German carpenter, Bruno Richard Hauptmann, really the man who kidnapped and killed the Lindbergh baby?

Charles Lindbergh, Jr., the kidnap victim.

To answer this question, the FBI once more opens its mammoth file on the Lindbergh case containing over 83 volumes, and reveals the principal facts from the day of the kidnapping on March 1, 1932, to the final arrest and conviction of Hauptmann.

Little did the wife of the world-famous aviator Charles A. Lindbergh realize as she tucked blond, blue-eyed Charles, Junior, into his crib on that fateful evening in March, 1932, that this was to be the last time she would ever see him alive.

She fretted about the cold which tormented the twenty-month-old baby and tenderly drew the warm blankets about him to fasten them down snugly with safety pins. The nurse had carefully locked all the windows in the nursery except the north window, directly opposite the crib, which was left open for proper ventilation. The young mother lingered in the doorway, taking one last look at the sleeping child before she snapped off the light, plunging the pleasant little room into darkness. It was 7:30 P.M.

Colonel Lindbergh arrived home shortly afterwards and the happy couple settled down after dinner to enjoy a quiet evening at home. It was almost 10 P.M. when the first shadows of the impending tragedy loomed over the Lindbergh home. Colonel Lindbergh had been looking over some papers in the living room when the frightened voice of Mrs. Lindbergh called to him, asking if he had taken the baby from its crib.

Dashing up the stairs past his wife and the baby's nurse, he switched on the nursery light. The crib was empty; only the crumpled blankets bespoke its former occupant. As the anxious father searched the room frantically in a wild hope that his son had perhaps climbed out of the crib and hid nearby, he discovered a note lying prominently on the window sill. The crude scrawl read; "Have $50,000 ready. The child is in gut care. We warn you for making anything public or for notify the police."

By eleven o'clock of that evening, the Lindbergh home at Hopewell, New Jersey, ablaze with lights, was being searched from top to bottom by the authorities; the help, questioned, and the startling news was being flashed across the country by radio, telegraph, and telephone. Extras, peddled by excited newsboys along the darkened streets of many cities, proclaimed in bold black type: "LINDBERGH BABY Kidnapped. CHARLES LINDBERGH, JR., MISSING FROM HOPEWELL HOME."

Meanwhile, the authorities were endeavoring to trace down every clue which might give some hint as to the identity of the kidnapper or kidnappers. It was determined that the kidnapping, itself, must have taken place sometime between eight and ten in the evening. Traces of mud were found on the floor of the nursery. An important clue—later to incriminate Hauptmann gravely—was a three-section ladder found about fifty feet from the house. Two sections of the ladder had been used in reaching the window, one of the two sections being split or broken during the descent. There were no blood stains in or about the nursery and examination failed to reveal any fingerprints. The household and estate employees, after being questioned, were investigated thoroughly and all were cleared of suspicion.

For four long days while the kidnapper kept a grim silence, shreds of evidence were fitted together—slowly, painstakingly—until they formed a pattern which enabled the authorities to visualize the actual kidnapping. Sometime during those two hours while the Lindbergh household was occupied on the ground floor, while Charles, Jr., was sleeping peacefully in his crib, the kidnapper had placed the ladder under the nursery window and scaled it noiselessly. He had picked up the infant, clad in its one-piece coverall night suit, and after propping the ransom note on the window sill, had begun the dangerous descent. The ladder had broken during that descent, causing the kidnapper to drop his precious bundle. Whether the child had been seriously injured could not be determined since there were no blood stains on the ground or along the side of the house. The frantic parents and the authorities could only hope that the kidnapper would be humane enough to seek medical attention for the infant if it were necessary, and they made widespread appeals to start negotiations. The baby's diet and the hither-to-unknown fact that the baby had been ill with a cold were published in the papers.

FIRST CONTACT WITH THE KIDNAPPER

Finally on March 6, 1932, Colonel Lindbergh received a second ransom note, postmarked Brooklyn, New York, increasing the ransom to $70,000 and declaring that the baby was well and would be fed according to his diet. With expectant hope he prepared the ransom money confident that his efforts would result in the swift return of the baby.

When an elderly, retired school principal, Dr. John F. Condon, ("Jafsie"), of the Bronx, New York City, published an offer in the "Bronx Home News" to act as go-between and to add $1,000 of his savings to the ransom, the family gratefully accepted his offer after the kidnapper had signified through another note that he would be willing to accept Condon as the intermediary.

For four weeks the kidnapper corresponded with the school principal advising as to the preparations for delivering the ransom money, even drawing a sketch of a certain type of box in which the money was to be placed. This sketch, later to add another irrevocable link to the chain of evidence convicting Hauptmann, helped the authorities to build up a mental picture of the kidnapper. The drawing itself with its exact dimensions, placed outside the lines, indicated that the man they were looking for had some knowledge of blueprints. He was either an architect or a craftsman of some type.

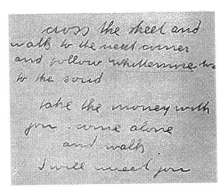

Ransom note instructing time and place for final payoff.

The crude sentence structure and the vocabulary of the kidnapper—peculiarized by his correct spelling of long, difficult words and foreign spelling of shorter and simpler words— discounted an architect or similarly educated American and seemed to indicate strongly that the kidnapper was of some foreign extraction, possibly German, who apparently consulted the dictionary to write out long, unfamiliar words and resorted to his own native pronunciation and spelling for the more commonly used words e.g., "gut" for good in the ransom notes.

DR. CONDON MEETS THE KIDNAPPER

In the meantime, the kidnapper who called himself "John," met Dr. Condon in a deserted section of a cemetery in the Bronx, New York, on March 12, 1932, and discussed payment of the ransom. He reassured the Doctor in guttural tones that the baby was well and that he would send its sleeping suit as a token of identity. He also cautioned absolute secrecy as to future negotiations.

The long, weary period of waiting seemed to be almost over for the anxious parents when Dr. Condon, following instructions from a previous note, found the twelfth ransom note under a stone in front of a greenhouse in the Bronx, April 2, 1932, instructing him to meet "John" that evening in St. Raymond's Cemetery, Bronx, for payment of the ransom. While the Lindberghs waited hopefully, Dr. Condon met "John" that evening and persuaded him to reduce the demand to $50,000. After receipt of the thirteenth note, purporting to contain information as to where the baby could be found, Dr. Condon gave "John" the $50,000. The stranger, clutching his ill-gotten wealth under his arm, then disappeared into the nearby woods.

The last ransom note. This was handed to Dr. Condon at the time the $50,000 in ransom money was given to "John." This message led Colonel Lindbergh and his wife to believe they would soon have their baby safely again.

The note which the elderly doctor had accepted in such good faith when read by Colonel Lindbergh advised, "The boy is on *Boad* Nelly—it is a small *Boad* 28 feet long, two persons are on the *Boad. the* are *innosent.* you will find the *Boad* between Horseneck Beach and Gay Head near Elizabeth Island."

Many will remember with compassion the search which was then made—the search for the boat named "Nellie" near Martha's Vineyard, Massachusetts—the search for the curly-headed youngster with the dimpled chin and smiling eyes. But all efforts were fruitless; Charles Lindbergh, Jr. was nowhere to be found. The kidnapper had disappeared with his money leaving only a mocking, false trail for the broken-hearted parents to pursue.

THE BABY'S BODY FOUND

On May 12, 1932, what had been a growing premonition on the part of the authorities became a stark reality when the body of Charles Lindbergh, Jr., was discovered accidentally by William Allen, a black truck assistant, partially buried in the shrubs, badly decomposed, about four and a half miles southeast of the Lindbergh home near Mount Rose, New Jersey. The body was 45 feet from the highway. The head was crushed; a hole in the skull had been made by a hammer or some other blunt instrument in the hands of the murderer. Some of the body members were missing. The remains were positively identified by Colonel Lindbergh and the baby's nurse. The Coroner's examination disclosed that the child had been dead for about two months and that death was caused by a blow on the head.

On the day following the finding of the baby's body, the President personally requested the Federal Bureau of Investigation to serve as a clearinghouse and coordinating agency for all investigations in this case conducted by Federal units and issued Presidential Instructions that all Governmental investigative agencies should place themselves at the disposal of the State of New Jersey. Prior to this time the FBI had acted merely in an auxiliary capacity due to lack of federal jurisdiction and had confined its investigative activities largely to inquiries specifically requested by the State of New Jersey.

On May 23, 1932, the FBI notified all banking institutions that it was now the coordinating agency for all governmental activity in the case and requested them to keep a close watch for the ransom money.

Under Mr. Hoover's direction, the FBI marshalled its investigative forces into a powerful, swiftly moving, cooperative drive to ferret out the murderer of the Lindbergh baby. In order to prevent duplication of investigations, the Bureau transmitted copies of all its investigations in this case to the other interested police agencies—New Jersey State Police and the New York City Police—which agreed, in turn, to submit copies of their investigative activities to the FBI.

In the process of accumulating, studying and analyzing all known facts and evidence in the case, the FBI Laboratory alone conducted well over one hundred document examinations, in addition to paper comparisons, blood tests, and examinations of typewritten documents. After meticulous examination of the ransom notes, handwriting experts unanimously concurred that all the notes were written by the same person and that the writer was of German nationality who had spent considerable time in America.

INVESTIGATIVE MACHINERY IN ACTION

In order to have a more clearly defined mental picture of "John," Special Agents engaged Dr. Condon to prepare a transcript of all conversations had by him with "John." These conversations, transcribed in detail on phonograph records, imitated the pronunciation and dialect of "John" and in this manner the nationality, education, mentality and character of the suspected kidnapper were brought more sharply into focus.

Sketches of "John" who received the Lindbergh kidnap ransom money. These were drawn for the FBI by James T. Berryman, staff artist of the Washington, D.C. Evening Star. He based the sketches on the verbal description given by Dr. John F. Condon and Joseph Perrone.

The FBI also retained the services of an artist to prepare a sketch of "John" from descriptions furnished by Dr. Condon and by Joseph Perrone, a taxicab driver who had delivered one of the ransom letters to Dr. Condon. Copies of this sketch were used to advantage by Agents when they combed sections of New York City where some of the ransom bills had been passed.

As the weeks wore into months, the popular sentiment of the nation fluctuated from primary shock to sympathy for the grief-stricken parents, and finally to righteous indignation, resulting in a deluge of letters storming the FBI. On a whole these letters were sincere and well-meant but many were written by publicity seekers, frauds and demented persons. It was essential, however, that all possible clues, regardless of the prospect of success, be carefully followed, since it was impossible in the vast majority of instances to determine at the inception whether they would be material or false. Thus, the FBI spent innumerable months tracing down the source of each letter, investigating every rumor, every claim, to its origin.

The President's Proclamation requiring the return to the Treasury of all gold and gold certificates was of invaluable assistance at this time since $40,000.00 of the ransom money had been paid in gold certificates and at the time of the Proclamation a large portion of this money was known to be outstanding.

Therefore, the FBI again emphasized this phase of the investigation by issuing a circular letter on January 17, 1934, to all banks and their branches in New York City, requesting an extremely close watch for the ransom certificates. Copies of a revised pamphlet containing the serial numbers of ransom bills and currency key cards—setting forth the inclusive serial numbers of all the ransom notes which had been paid—were distributed by Special Agents to each employee handling currency in banks, clearinghouses, grocery stores in certain selected communities, insurance companies, gasoline filling stations, airports, department stores, post offices and telegraph companies.

Six months later, on August 20, 1934, the FBI's carefully planned trap sprung. Starting on this date and extending into September, a total of sixteen gold certificates, all ransom bills, were discovered in the vicinity of Yorkville and Harlem. As each bill was recovered, Special Agents inserted a colored pin, denoting the location of the recovery, in a large map of the Metropolitan Area, thus indicating the movement of the individual who was passing the ransom money. Teams composed of Special Agents and representatives of the interested police agencies combed the districts where the bills were first caught and personally urged the banks to redouble their efforts to determine the original depositor. In this manner, for the first time in the history of the case, the investigators were able to question the individuals who received the ransom bills and obtain a description of the "stranger" passing the bills.

The trail grew warmer and warmer as the FBI tightened its dragnet around New York City. Descriptions of the "stranger" tallied exactly with that of "John." Fruit dealers, grocers, shoe salesmen—all remembered the fair-haired man with the foreign accent and the pointed chin who had offered ten and twenty dollar gold certificates for minor purchases.

BREAKING THE CASE

On September 18, 1934, the Assistant Manager of the Corn Exchange Bank and Trust Company in Harlem telephoned the New York Office and advised that a ten dollar gold certificate had been discovered a few minutes previously by one of the tellers in the bank.

Immediately, Special Agents with representatives of the police agencies, made a thorough check and ascertained that this bill had been received at the Bank from a gasoline filling station located at 127th Street and Lexington Avenue.

Events moved swiftly from that time on as the investigating squad questioned the alert gas attendant who had received the bill in payment for five gallons of gasoline. Questioning the validity of the gold certificate, the attendant had taken the precaution to record on the bill the license number of the car driven by the stranger. With increasing excitement—the authorities listened to the description of the purchaser—a man of Scandinavian appearance, foreign accent, fair complexion. When the attendant had eyed the bill dubiously, the stranger had remarked that the bill was good all right and that he had 100 more just like that.

Telephone wires began to hum as the license number was checked. The authorities waited with bated breath as the information came over the wire. The name of the man to whom license 4 U 13-41 had been issued was Bruno Richard Hauptmann of 1279 East 222nd St., Bronx, New York.

That night while Special Agents and representatives of the New Jersey and New York police agencies were keeping a close watch on the two-story house, located at the corner of a sparsely settled German section—one block from the Boston Post Road, technicians of the FBI Laboratory were busily engaged in comparing photostatic copies of the suspect's automobile registration and driver's license with the ransom notes. Other Agents were rounding up information on the suspect: Bruno Richard Hauptmann, apparently unemployed, married, father of one male child, German nationality, 35, carpenter by trade.

All descriptions tallied with the physical features of the man sought for more than two years as the possible kidnapper and murderer of the Lindbergh baby.

At approximately 9:00 the following morning, the suspect emerged from the house and entered his garage where he kept a Dodge sedan. As he drove rapidly down Park Avenue followed closely behind by the authorities, he little suspected that the sands of time were running out for him—this was Judgment Day!

At Park Avenue, near 178th Street—the authorities closed in and forced the suspect to the side of the road. As they surrounded the Dodge, Agents quickly realized that the driver of the car was the perfect image of the sketch made from the description of "John" furnished by Dr. Condon. When searched, a twenty dollar gold ransom certificate was found on his person.

As the investigation of the German carpenter progressed rapidly in the ensuing days, the FBI became more and more confident that this was the man responsible not only for collecting the ransom money but also for the kidnapping and murder of the Lindbergh baby. Dr. Condon and the taxicab driver positively identified Hauptmann as "John" who had negotiated the ransom transactions.

The Hauptmann garage which contained the ransom money.

In searching the Hauptmann house and surrounding grounds, incriminating evidence slowly mounted up—forming an impregnable case against Hauptmann. A pair of shoes purchased with a twenty dollar ransom bill, recovered on September 8, 1934, was found. The address and telephone number of Dr. Condon were also found written in pencil on the door; and there were several scribbled notations which proved to be certain serials of the ransom money. Packages of the ransom money itself—wrapped in newspapers—totalling $13,760.00 were found hidden in the garage. The 1931 Dodge sedan belonging to Hauptmann answered exactly to the description of the car seen in the vicinity of the Lindbergh home the day prior to the kidnapping.

Handwriting experts of the FBI Laboratory positively identified Hauptmann's handwriting as being the same as the handwriting on the ransom notes.

In the midst of the government investigation official reports from Hauptmann's native country, Germany, began to come in:

Bruno Richard Hauptmann, German alien, who
entered the United States illegally in 1923.

"Bruno Richard Hauptmann—35, native of Saxony, Germany, where, on March 6, 1919, in the town of Kamenz, he was sentenced on a charge of joint great robbery to serve a sentence of two years and six months imprisonment and four years loss of civil rights. Also sentenced on a charge of joint highway robbery to serve two years and three months in prison and to suffer the loss of civil rights for two years. Served four years of this term and was released pending his good behavior."

Additional investigation revealed that early in July, 1923, Hauptmann had stowed away aboard the SS Hanover at Bremen, Germany, arrived in the port of New York City on July 13, 1923, and successfully made an illegal entry. On October 10, 1925,

Hauptmann married Anna Schoeffler, a New York City waitress. A son, Manfried, was born to them in 1933. During his illegal stay in New York City and until the spring of 1932, Hauptmann followed his occupation of carpenter. However, a short while after March 1, 1932, the date of the kidnapping, Hauptmann began to trade rather extensively in stocks and ceased the practice of his carpentry trade.

Interior of the Hauptmann garage. Here the kidnapper had buried $13,760 of the ransom money.

THE FINAL CHAPTER

Bruno Richard Hauptmann was indicted in the Supreme Court, Bronx County, New York, on charges of extortion on September 26, 1934, and October 8, 1934, in Hunterdon County, New Jersey, he was indicted for murder. Two days later on October 10, 1934, the Governor of the State of New York honored the requisition of the Governor of the State of New Jersey for the surrender of Hauptmann and on October 19, 1934, he was removed to the Hunterdon County Jail, Flemington, New Jersey, to await trial.

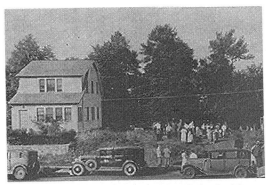

The Hauptmann home. A portion of the ladder used in
the kidnapping was taken from the attic timbers of this house.

During the ensuing five weeks' trial the FBI extended every
cooperation to the State of New Jersey. Additional evidence,
strongly implicating the accused, was brought out during the trial.
A government wood expert testified that prior to the arrest of
Hauptmann he had traced the wood used in the construction of
the kidnapping ladder from a mill in South Carolina to a lumber
company in the Bronx, New York. It was definitely ascertained that
Hauptmann had purchased wood from this lumber company. The
expert also identified a piece of wood missing from Hauptmann's
attic as being one of the side rails of the ladder. He further proved
that the plane owned by the accused was used in making the
ladder. Further damaging evidence was the chisel found at the
scene of the kidnapping which, according to the wood expert, was
used in the manufacture of the ladder and which at the time of the
accused's apprehension was found to fit perfectly into his tool kit
from which a chisel was missing.

On February 13, 1935, Bruno Richard Hauptmann was found
guilty and sentenced by the Court to be executed. On April 3,
1936, at 8:47 P.M. the man found by a Jury of his peers to be
responsible for the kidnapping and murder of the twenty-month-
old baby, Charles Lindbergh, Jr., was electrocuted.

Kansas City Massacre

We are prone to forget that in the 1930s and 1940s we were living in the great gang age—that bloody era when organized gangsterism threatened to tilt the balance between crime and law. It was the age when FBI Agents were not authorized to carry guns; when prison breaks were commonplace; when corrupt bosses kept the heat off vicious killers and provided them with "cooling off" spots. It was the age when machine guns were sold for hard cash and no questions asked; when the airplane, automobile and telephone allowed the members of an invisible empire to laugh at the law. This was the setting for a crime that shocked the nation—the Kansas City Massacre.

When the heat was on, the rat-eyed small shots might scuttle to their holes and lie in fear and hiding. Not so the big-time boy. He knew where to go. No skulking for him. Luxury, safety, a Chief of Detectives who not only shut his eyes to others' failings but who indulged in a few little rackets of his own like selling diamonds to inhabitants of disorderly houses. And to top that, there was a political machine providing protection and grinding out gangland favors with a swish of greased palms and the oily grace of a squat little boss.

Such was Hot Springs, Arkansas.

Frank Nash

Frank Nash, murderer, train-robber, graduate of McAlester penitentiary, fled out of the rear door of a Leavenworth warden's home into freedom. He had served six years of a twenty-five year term when he made his break from the Federal prison on October 19, 1930. Nash scuttled back to the desolate Cookson Hills in Oklahoma to establish old connections. There he waited for the heat to die down, and then, armed with letters of introduction, trekked up to St. Paul, Minnesota.

This outpost of the underworld empire was ruled by "Ma" Barker, her son Fred and Verne Miller—a willow-spined character who had learned the intricacies of machine gunning in France and now enjoyed cuddling a chattering gun to further his career in crime.

Nash was highly welcome in Minnesota. He told the St. Paul gang lords about the safety of his Oklahoma bad lands. Soon he had opened the old-time-outlaw-infested Cooksons to a streamlined variety of bandit. There, he said, was the ideal cooling-off spot, the hoodlum's haven. They were inaccessible and safe and just across the way was Paradise—Hot Springs, Arkansas.

But there was a fly in the ointment—too many bosom pals were absent, detained by John law. It was a situation the empire knew how to remedy.

On the morning of December 11, 1931, seven prisoners broke out of Leavenworth Penitentiary. They kidnapped and wounded the warden. In the background hovered the balding, hook-nosed Nash, furnishing firearms, welcoming them to the Cooksons.

More were coming. On Memorial Day, May 30, 1933, six

convicts disrupted a baseball game in the yard of the Kansas State penitentiary, kidnapped the warden and escaped. They were a deadly gang: Wilbur Underhill, Harvey Bailey, Robert Brady, Ed Davis, Jim Clark and Fred Purell.

It was like old home week in the Oklahoma hills. Frank Nash welcomed his Empire friends.

Of course Nash had changed. Now he wore a smart new toupee on his shiny pate; he had grown a moustache. He hurried about the Cooksons settling his guests; making them comfortable in their crude quarters. They might in time get bored—but across the line and inland such a little way was gangland's Utopia. He went there often. There was the White Front Pool Hall under the partial proprietorship of Good Friend Galatas. Solid Citizen Galatas. Galatas of the Gang whose hand rested on the web that sent warning messages to the Empire. Peace and quiet and safety at the White Front....

APPREHENDING A DANGEROUS FUGITIVE

It was June 16, 1933, when this pool room sanctuary suddenly felt the presence of men who lacked the swaggering gait of gangster gunmen.

Frank Nash felt his arms clamped tightly at his sides. He heard low authoritative voices "Agents of the FBI.... authority of the Attorney General ... Leavenworth."

The safety of the White Front was no more. Almost instantly he was in a speeding car. He was leaving freedom, safety, and Hot Springs. Galatas had been there. He'd known what to do. Just get in touch with the big shots, pull the switch; the machinery of the Empire would go into action. Con-man Galatas hurried to the home of Mrs. Conner. Mrs. Conner's phone bill rose steadily. A call to the O. P. Inn, gang center in Chicago. Quick: Tell Louis Stacci the Feds got Frank. Ask what to do.

A crooked "guardian" of the law, the super sleuth of Hot Springs, went into action.

This good friend of the gang sent out a state-wide call that a man had been kidnapped from the White Front Pool Hall. The order went out for officers to stop the "kidnappers" and release the victim! And back of this command in the name of law and order was a squat little political boss whose corrupt rule guarded the Empire.

Three grim-faced men, two Agents and Chief of Police Reed of McAlester, Oklahoma, knew they were facing more than a handful of rat-faced killers. They were dealing with Organized Crime backed by Corrupt Politics and Public Indifference.

Once they had the scrawny killer in their waiting auto they swung the car toward Little Rock and stepped on the gas. They were dealing with life and death and Gangland.

A few miles out, roaring sirens stopped them. No, this man is not being kidnapped. This is Frank Nash, killer, Federal Prisoner. We are returning him to Leavenworth to complete a 25 year sentence. Identification? The bright gold badges of the FBI. This is the Federal government.

They were allowed to proceed but they knew what they faced. They had to get Nash out of there.

Back in Hot Springs long distance wires were burning. In Chicago, Louis (Doc) Stacci listened to the news of "Jelly" Nash's arrest. His orders snapped along the wires. "Find Verne Miller in K.C."

The Agents slowed down long enough to check with their superiors. The Federal Government knew it was battling dynamite—and it was fighting with its hands tied against an octopus-like opponent.

"Get rid of your car. Get that man on a train. Look out for an ambush."

They were stopped again. This time at Little Rock. It was the same story. Their man was a Federal Prisoner, not a kidnap victim. Where were they taking him? Joplin, Missouri, and from there to Leavenworth.

Their questioners let them go, escorted them to the highway leading to Joplin, and left them.

Some miles out of Little Rock the road divides. One branch

goes toward Joplin, Missouri; one toward Fort Smith, Arkansas.

The car carrying Frank Nash turned toward Fort Smith, Arkansas.

The hands of the clock raced on into late afternoon that tense sixteenth day of June, 1933. It was only a few hours after Stacci's orders snapped over the wire from Chicago. A plane fluttered over the Joplin airport, settled, rolled to a stop—and out stepped Richard Galatas and Mrs. Frank Nash! A 16-cylinder car driven by ex-convict Herbert Farmer roared up to whisk them off.

Soon the telephone wires were hot again—Stacci in Chicago to Miller in Kansas City to the waiting group in Joplin ... But the Empire found there had been a slip up. There was that clever turn to Fort Smith ... Frank Nash and his captors never showed up in Joplin....

There were hurried phone calls. The underground Empire wasn't stopping. Frank was a pal, a good contact to have in the Cooksons, and Verne Miller, ex-Sheriff from Huron, South Dakota, arrested in office for embezzlement, now turned trigger-man for the Empire, had his orders. But the job was big. He needed help and the thugs he knew weren't blessed with courage. Then out of the south came unexpected aid. On the morning of June 16, 1933, Sheriff Jack Killingsworth had walked into a local garage in Bolivar, Missouri. Two men eyed suspiciously. One was coarse featured, stocky; the other, slim, dark, olive-skinned, furtive.

Recognition was swift. "Pretty Boy" Floyd and his follower Adam Richetti! Before the sheriff could move he was covered, hustled into a car and forced to obey the deadly pair.

Then began a wild ride. A second man was snatched; another car stolen.

The sheriff was released about eight o'clock that evening when the ride ended in Kansas City.

Here was heaven-sent aid! Neither Floyd nor Richetti was long on brains but both had eager trigger fingers; both were reckless; both hated the law.

Miller flashed out a request for gunmen. The answer came back. Sure! Glad to help. Anything for a pal.

An aerial view of the Union Railroad Station,
Kansas City, Missouri.

DEATH ON A JUNE DAY

The morning sun glinted brightly down on Kansas City's huge Union Station. There was the usual sudden buzz of excitement before the arrival of each train. The 7:12 was due any minute.

A fair sized crowd was there to meet it. In the group a little cluster of quiet watchful-eyed men waited alert and patient. The Special Agent in Charge of the Kansas City Division, a second FBI Agent and two Kansas City Police Officers were on hand to see that Federal Prisoner Frank Nash went safely on his way to Leavenworth.

The 7:12 finally puffed in. The two Agents and Chief Reed led their manacled prisoner off the train, through the concourse. They were greeted by the waiting group. There must be no delay. They walked quickly through the depot, onto the plaza and up to the car that would take Frank Nash sixteen miles up the river.

The sun poured down throwing long, early morning shadows. Traffic eddied about in an endless stream.

Frank Nash was placed in the rear seat of the automobile. Then for some reason there was a change; a swift decision to put Nash in the front seat. Obediently he slid under the wheel while the split front seat was placed forward to allow the officers to enter the back of the car. The Special Agent in Charge and the two police officers stood watch. Agent Caffrey was about to enter the car.

Suddenly there was a blur of sound; of split-second action; voices.

"Up! Up! Get 'em up!" No one waited for the command to be obeyed. "Let 'em have it!"

A machine gun began its deadly chatter. The popping of a .38 and the louder blast of a .45 caliber revolver were lost in the steady staccato bark of the big gun.

The Kansas City detectives slumped down side by side. Agent Caffrey dropped on the opposite side of the car. The Agent in Charge fell wounded and crawled behind the machine.

Slugs tore through the car. Steadily, deliberately, the assassins made a brief quarter circle, spraying the car with lead.

One Agent writhed to the floor, his back torn with bullets. Chief Otto Reed slumped forward, dead. In the front seat behind the wheel Frank Nash's head fell back. Bullets cut through his neck. The new toupee fell off, stained with bright blood.

"We shot Nash!"

"They're all dead. Let's go!"

There was a sudden silence on the plaza, stunned unbelievable silence that lasted several seconds. Then there was movement. People crawled from beneath cars. Machines started. There was an excited eddying mass and the killers merged with the crowd, entered their car and disappeared. The FBI Agent in Charge, shot in the arm, thrust through the crowd to put in a riot call.

Four officers were dead: Agent Caffrey, Detectives Groom and Hermanson, and Chief Otto Reed.

An FBI Agent occupying the center of the back seat where a prisoner would normally sit, was untouched. He was applying first aid to a wounded Agent when traffic parted for a clanging ambulance.

Frank Nash was dead. The Empire had sprung him from captivity in life to captivity in death and in so doing, had lost its greatest ally—Public Indifference. The sleeping citizenry awakened startled. Here was mass murder. Here was organized crime flaunting itself in the face of the whole nation. Hadn't everyone said it was a good thing to have gang wars? Let them kill each other off? But here were gangster's guns spurting streams of death at guardians of the law.

From Washington came the terse order, "Get them!"

SECRETS OF THE UNDERWORLD

Within hours the series of phone calls plotting the delivery had been traced—from Galatas to Stacci to Miller.... But who were the killers?

Agents of the FBI cracked down on Verne Miller's Kansas City home. He was gone. Gone, too, was thin-faced Vivian Mathis, his cold-eyed paramour.

Out of the place came everything that might yield a clue; clothes, papers, glasses, an empty beer bottle....

Out came dusting powders, iodine tests, cameras.

And on the empty beer bottle in the home of Vernon Miller a fingerprint appeared. The fingerprint was not Miller's....

Verne C. Miller

Adam Richetti

It was axiomatic that where Charles Arthur "Pretty Boy" Floyd went, there went Adam Richetti. It worked in reverse. Where Adam Richetti went, there went "Pretty Boy" Floyd.

"Pretty Boy" Floyd

The fingerprint on the empty beer bottle in the home of suspect Miller was the fingerprint of Adam Richetti.

Where did the killers go? Kansas City was hot; so hot that every underworld character ducked for a hideout. The Empire shut up shop like a "dead" possum. Kansas City looked like it might have harbored a pestilence. But there was always Chicago.

Verne Miller was scuttling into the Chicago suburbs the very moment FBI Agents were checking the Kansas City apartment which he had rented in the name of Vincent C. Moore, and then acquitted so unceremoniously.

Boldly he braked his car before a Maywood Apartment, knocked lightly, was admitted. Moments later he emerged with a youthful curly-haired man. The latter was nervous, apprehensive. The pair put the car in the garage and re-entered the house.

For four days Verne Miller, joined by Vi Mathis, hid out with Volney Davis and Edna Murray.

Davis, a member of the Barker-Karpis mob, and his gun, didn't relish the idea of open house to anyone as hot as Miller—or possibly their jittery state of mind was induced by the fact that on the day preceding the Massacre their own gang had pulled the Harem kidnapping in St. Paul.

Whatever the reason, Miller and Vivian were hurried to the airport, boarded a plane and took off for New York.

FUGITIVES IN FLIGHT

This marked the split in the trail. Pretty Boy Floyd and Adam Richetti broke away, twisted and turned, back tracked; finally going into hiding so complete that they might have dropped from the face of the earth.

Quiet, solemn-faced men with FBI shields slipped in and out of underworld haunts. No hint in the papers to tell how they were doing. Just that careful, continuous painstaking search.

Where were they? Kingpins of the underworld knew they were sweating out the long minutes, hours, and days in a six room apartment in Buffalo, New York.

They were not alone. Rose and Juanita Baird shared their imprisonment.

Back in Oklahoma, Rose and Juanita had joined up with two hometown hoodlums. Rose had married Wallace Ash; Juanita lived with his brother. Then one day the coarse-featured sisters met "Pretty Boy" Floyd and a pal. They were interested, and conveniently enough the Ash brothers, small time stuff in the criminal log, soon afterwards found themselves enveloped in a hail of hot lead. Their women passed into stronger hands.

Somewhere along the route of flight from the bloody Union Station to Toledo, Ohio, Floyd and Richetti were joined by Rose and Juanita Baird. They raced on to Buffalo.

In their hideout the foursome settled down to a quiet life. So quiet that it was maddening. Day after day the once dapper Richetti sat with his head in his hands, morose and sullen. He seldom spoke. Anger flared over his stolid silence.

Floyd was not one to sit still. Day and night in his waking hours he paced back and forth, back and forth, like a caged animal.

"That guy's driving me loopy," remarked the occupant of a lower apartment. Neighbors felt something was wrong. No telephone: no friends; no one leaving the house but for brief nocturnal visits to the grocer's. Occasionally one of the heavy-featured girls broke the boredom by tossing coins to neighborhood children from the windows or sought their friendship by offering them candy.

For 13 months they were holed up in their prison-like apartment. But they couldn't stand it any longer.

When Pretty Boy said, "Who wants to go home?" the answer was an excited chorus.

He gave the girls money to buy a car. Mr. and Mrs. "George Sanders" and Mr. and Mrs. "Eddie Brennen" were leaving the apartment; leaving town going back to the Cooksons—and the quicker they got there the better....

Under cover of a thick fog their car sped through the dark streets of Buffalo, headed west. The sleepy occupants were quite content. At last they were going home.

PERSONA NON GRATA

On the day following the Massacre Mrs. Conner, whose phone had been used, left Hot Springs. Galatas fled. There was a flurry in the Underworld. The crime engineers were being rounded up—Herbert Farmer, "Doc" Stacci, Frank Mulloy who had relayed Stacci's message to her, and later Richard Tallman Galatas. The Empire suffered nervous chills. Verne Miller found himself so hot he was an unwelcome guest even among old friends. He began to move, apprehensively.

On November 1, 1933, Verne Miller walked into a trap set by the G-Men. Agents had located Vivian Mathis in a Chicago Apartment house. They knew Miller must be close. The necessity of haste left one loophole and before it could be closed Miller escaped through a hail of lead; Vivian Mathis was arrested.

The hunt was on again. Once more the tireless Agents began sifting and screening and fitting together the incredibly minute pieces of the mosaic that makes a criminal pattern. Telephone calls, a ticket stub, a hotel register, a trickle of rumor ... They were close behind him. They knew where he had been—the day, the hour ... and the gap was closing.

The faint little sounds echoed out of the underworld—Miller was broke and desperate. He had to have money and his gun was for hire. Price? Five hundred for one; three for a thousand. Between November 26 and 28, 1933, three of Detroit's public enemies were blotted out by a machine gunner whose technique was individual and expert. The rumors increased. They gave Miller the credit.

Up in Connecticut on November 20, the body of Al Silvers, traveling representative of the Longie Zwillman mob in control of New Jersey's underworld, was found along a highway, feet hooked over a barbed wire fence. He had been garroted, beaten, stabbed with a blunt-nosed knife, wrapped in cheap blankets and bound with new clothesline rope drawn cruelly tight. He was nude but for a tightly drawn rope about his neck concealed by an impeccable four-in-hand tie.

What had Silvers done?

Rumor said he had befriended Miller; had arranged for him to pose as a traveling salesman for a New Jersey optical concern; and had bought the Ford car which Miller drove to Chicago and abandoned in the battle at the apartment house.

This had turned the "G-Heat" Jersey-ward. The mob big shots didn't like it. Louie Puchalter, kingpin of the New York City rackets, didn't like it, notwithstanding the fact that his wife had offered haven to Vi Mathis while Agents hunted for her. The word went out that Silvers was on the rub-out list—and anyone else who befriended Miller. The Empire was feeling the heat and Miller was *persona non grata*.

On November 29, 1933, a message reached the FBI. The headlights of a car fell on an oddly wrapped bundle in a vacant lot. It was almost covered with marsh grass. The driver reported the incident.

Police investigated. Under a cheap automobile robe, wrapped in cheap blankets, knees cramped horribly, bound by new clothesline rope, was the nude body of a murdered man. He had been strangled. Eleven wounds showed that he had been cruelly beaten with a blunt instrument. He had been hammered and shot to death as he slept or as he lay in a drunken stupor.

The dead man's fingerprints were sent to the FBI files. It was Verne Miller.

So Miller was done for. Floyd had read it in the Buffalo papers. Richetti sneered, "Crazy fool should have stayed hid."

"PRETTY BOY" FLOYD

Eleven months later they thought of him as they cruised down the highway for safety, security and the Cooksons. Suddenly out of the fog loomed strange objects—a pole and fence. Brakes screeched. The car crashed.

Floyd and Richetti picked themselves out of a ditch. The women were scared but unhurt. It was October 21, 1934, and daybreak was only an hour away. Hastily they removed their arsenal from the wreck, sent one of the girls to town for a wrecker and hid in the woods.

There wasn't much time left for the Kansas City Killers. Shortly reports were turned in to local officers that two suspicious-looking men were noted on the outskirts of Wellsville, Ohio.

Officers went out to investigate. As they closed in, the two fugitives came up shooting. Richetti was apprehended but Floyd escaped. Then an alarm went out. The whole community was alert. The territory was surrounded. The following day "Pretty Boy" was seen on a farm near Clarkson, Ohio. Four Agents and four local officers sped to the scene. As they approached, the bandit from the Cooksons started running. "Halt! FBI!" He didn't stop.

Bullets thudded after him. Floyd fell less than 60 yards away. The arresting officers came up cautiously with guns raised.

A cocked .45 caliber Colt automatic pistol was taken from the bandit's right hand. Its duplicate was thrust in his belt.

"I'm done for. You hit me twice," he gasped. More than a dozen bullets had struck him. The dying man gave his name as "Murphy," then admitted he was lying. This was the killer all right. The Agents knew he was Floyd, Charles Arthur Floyd.

When asked if he, Richetti and Miller had done the shooting at the Union Station, he answered, "I ain't tellin' you nothing," and a little later, "I'm going."

From his pocket fell a watch with a lucky piece chained to it. Both bore notches—ten on each. It was said these were symbols of murdered men—all killed by the Pretty Boy's guns. At 4:25 P.M. he was dead.

THE END OF THE ROAD

Frank Mulloy of the Horseshoe Tavern rendezvous in Kansas City, "Doc" Stacci of the "O. P. Inn" hangout in Chicago, Herb Farmer, the chicken rancher, and Galatas, the "finger" man, battled stubbornly to avoid the sentence imposed for conspiring to obstruct justice. Galatas had fled from pillar to post to avoid capture. After his arrest the unsavory group fought unsuccessfully to get clear. The corrupt political machine that harbored them was ineffective.

All four appealed to the United States Circuit Court of Appeals without effect. Three petitioned the United States Supreme Court which refused to review the case. Stacci began his time immediately; the others remained free on bond while prosecuting appeals and received two year sentences. Stacci's appeal for release by parole was denied.

Adam Richetti, trapped by his fingerprint, was the only member of the murderous trio to stand trial for the Union Station

Massacre. He was convicted and sentenced to be executed. At Jefferson City, Missouri, October 7, 1938, a lethal gas chamber opened to him. In a matter of minutes he was dead.

This was the beginning of the end. It was just as though the ridge pole in a huge Chautauqua tent had suddenly come smashing down.

The Empire was crumbling. Contacts were broken, communications were disrupted, gang lords had new forwarding addresses—Alcatraz, Leavenworth, Atlanta.... The organization and attention to detail of the Federal Bureau of Investigation, backed by cooperative police and an aroused public, was literally whittling the Empire to pieces.

Sixty-five volumes make up the file on the Kansas City Massacre. From the first teletype on the slaughter at Union Station to the last piece of mail the file is a story of patient, painstaking and tenacious probing by a few courageous investigators, striking a smashing blow against the swaggering, corrupt and sprawling Empire of Crime. The closed investigation of the Kansas City Massacre marks the twilight of the gangs.

The Barker-Karpis Gang

In the fabulous twenties, gangdom, like a malignant cancerous growth, insidiously took root in the heart of the nation, spreading so rapidly, that in the early thirties it lay an open festering sore—daily spawning new and more malevolent criminals who openly scoffed at law and order, punctuating their remarks with bursts of spraying lead.

The press had a name for them—"public enemies"—and they vied bitterly among themselves for this coveted title with its ensuing privileges—quick pardons, paroles, reprieves from unscrupulous politicians; unquestioning obedience from their underlings. They were little emperors ruling their territories with rods of steel—direct progenitors to the dynasties of John Dillinger, Pretty Boy Floyd, Baby Face Nelson, Frank Nash, Verne Miller, Adam Richetti and the like.

Such were the members of the notorious Barker-Karpis gang—"Ma" Barker with her four sons, Herman, Lloyd, Fred and Arthur; Alvin Karpis and their many criminal associates. Operating in the southwestern part of the United States at this time, they were arrogantly ravaging law-abiding society, ruthlessly plundering its wealth, and leaving a trail of death and destruction in their wake. Devotees of Epicureanism, they wallowed in a plethora of ill-gotten luxury; their creed—eat, drink and be merry for tomorrow who knows and who cares.

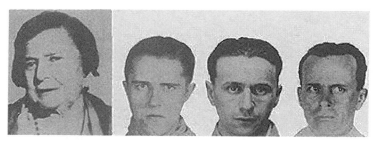

Left to right: Kate "Ma" Barker, Alvin Karpis, Fred Barker, Arthur Barker.

THE BRAINS OF THE GANG—"MA" BARKER

In order to appreciate the overwhelming power and influence of the Barker-Karpis gang, we must turn back the pages of time to the "gay nineties"—to the days when "mother was a girl" and Arizona Donnie Clark, nicknamed Kate for short, was in her teens.

Kate, a combination of Scotch, Irish and Indian extraction, enjoyed the social life of her community, the Ozark Mountains in the vicinity of Ashgrove, Missouri. Impulsive, loquacious, eager for life, she plunged enthusiastically into the numerous local activities. There were picnics, candy pulls, and pie socials in the little red school house. On summer evenings she and her companions could be found perched gaily on a rickety wagon, piled high with sweet-smelling hay, and being drawn along the moon-swept mountain trails by an old Missouri mule. On the Sabbath Day, blonde, blue-eyed Kate attended Sunday School and during the week, church socials and community sings. It was a normal happy girlhood, characteristic of the turn of the century, and it led to what appeared to be a normal happy womanhood. Kate married a childhood companion, George E. Barker, on September 14, 1892.

Early in married life while she was bearing her sons—Herman, Lloyd, Arthur and Freddie—Kate seemed content enough to be a good housewife whose chief fault was a leaning toward choice gossip about the neighbors and occasional fits of fanatical religious frenzy when she would engage in evangelistic activities.

As the novelty of marriage faded, however, and Kate Barker found herself faced with the grim realities of life, trying to feed, clothe and provide shelter for four children, she began to long for money—lots of it—enough to purchase extravagant clothing, expensive furniture and all sorts of luxuries which she knew her plodding husband could not provide on his meager salary. They were now barely existing in Tulsa, Oklahoma, to which town they had migrated after Herman, her oldest boy, had been arrested near Webb City, Missouri, in 1910. Although he had been released after being questioned, Kate had gone into a frenzied rage at the indignity to which her "poor, innocent boy" had been subjected. "We'll move out of this town," she had cried, and move they did, that is, all except Herman, proficient already in the art of highway robbery, Herman had ventured out into the world to seek his fame and fortune.

Top: Volney Davis, member of the Barker-Karpis gang, who received a sentence of life imprisonment in the United States Penitentiary at Alcatraz Island for his participation in the Bremer kidnapping.

Bottom: Edna Murray, Volney Davis' paramour, who escaped from the Missouri State Penitentiary three times before joining Davis and the Barker-Karpis gang. On her capture by the FBI, Edna Murray was returned to the Missouri State Penitentiary to complete the remainder of her 25-year sentence for highway robbery plus an additional two years for escaping in 1932.

"MA" BARKER'S SCHOOL FOR CRIME

Kate Barker's desire for wealth and power sharpened as the years rolled by, and her younger sons began to approach manhood. Inspired perhaps by Herman's unlawful but profitable activities, her quick, agile mind, aided by a native intelligence, began to plot ahead for the future. As she sat mending a three-cornered tear in Arthur's trousers or cutting down George's threadbare suit to fit Fred, her brain worked busily. Even if George Barker couldn't support her in the style she expected, her sons could. And would. Herman, Arthur, Lloyd, Fred—they'd take care of their "Ma"— they'd provide all the luxuries she craved so hungrily. She'd train them now when they were young and impressionable so that they'd know how later on! And so "Ma" Barker's school for crime began.

Under her brilliant tutelage, the young Barker boys flourished in the ways of the underworld. They joined the old Central Park gang in Tulsa, composed of the roughest, toughest hoodlums in the neighborhood. Their consorts were Sam Coker, Harry Campbell, Glenn Leroy Wright, Volney Davis....

PRELUDE TO UNDERWORLD POWER FOR "MA" BARKER AND THE BOYS

Frequently, the neighbors were forced to complain about "Ma's" boys as they progressed scholastically from boisterous rowdies to belligerent window breakers to sly petty thieves. However, when "Ma" was approached, she would wax indignant at the accusers and shout, "My boys can do no wrong. It's a lie."

Patiently, indomitably, "Ma" molded her sons into shrewd, cunning criminals. When they were first arrested for petty infractions of the law, she would descend on the police department the epitome of outraged motherhood. Tears, expostulations, and other sordid tactics would usually secure their release. If these failed, however, she would post their bond in order to protect their unsullied innocence and triumphantly cart them home where they would receive a bitter tongue lashing for being so stupid as to get caught.

If George Barker attempted to reprove and caution his sons for their misdoings, "Ma" would fly into a temper and berate him for interfering in her affairs. Meanwhile, "Mother" Barker's reputation was spreading in the underworld. Her home became a haven for her sons' gangster friends who affectionately called her "Ma." All were received with open arms; all sought her shrewd and sage advice. As her circle of acquaintances widened and developed, "Ma's" guest book began to list some of the most deadly outlaws of the day—"Pretty Boy" Floyd, "Baby Face" Nelson, Frank Nash, Verne Miller ... The hand that rocked the Barker boys' cradle was rapidly becoming the hand destined to be a ruling power in the southwest underworld.

The nineteen twenties found the Barker boys gravely pursuing their felonious careers with ambitious "Ma" in the background, constantly cautioning, counselling and collecting the spoils. Larceny, bank robbery, murder, they ran through the gamut of crime in rapid succession, daily acquiring new prestige in the eyes of the underworld. Harassed police were kept busy recording their latest depredations while local newspapers in the southwest were blasting for their apprehension.

As they fraternized freely with members of their profession, their underworld connections strengthened. They were introduced to shady citizens, willing to provide temporary haven while the heat was on for a slight compensation; to political bosses who winked an eye as they set in motion movements to secure quick acquittals and pardons. It was smooth sailing for "Ma" and her deadly brood; they had learned their childhood lessons well.

The law, however, was trailing close behind the Barkers, ready to close in at the first opportunity, and by the end of the twenties, it had succeeded in temporarily halting their crime crusade.

Herman Barker was dead. Rather than submit to an arrest on a charge of murdering a Kansas police officer, he had put a suicidal bullet through his own head. Curly-haired Arthur, more commonly known as "Doc," was imprisoned for life in the Oklahoma State Prison, charged with the murder of a night watchman during a robbery. Light-fingered Lloyd was "at home" for the next twenty-five years in the United States penitentiary at Leavenworth, Kansas, convicted of robbing the U.S. Mails. "Ma's" favorite, weasel-eyed Freddie, was quartered in the Kansas State Penitentiary on a five to ten-year sentence for burglary and larceny.

Although "Ma," comfortably plump and fortyish now, was distressed that her boys were temporarily being detained in jail, she continued to handle affairs on the outside and to formulate new plans for even greater glory when her boys came home. Discarding her husband, George, she showered her affections on a younger, more exciting lover, Arthur Dunlop—a man who could handle a gun capably on short notice, who said little and thought less.

To the remaining Barker boys this period of incarceration was regarded as just a lull between storms—an opportunity to take refresher courses in their selected profession; to renew old acquaintances; make new friends; meet worthwhile contacts.

Fred Barker became acquainted with slender, pleasant-featured Alvin Karpis, ten years his junior. The twenty-five-year-old Karpis, however, already had a substantial criminal record behind him. He had escaped from the State Industrial Reformatory at Hutchinson, Kansas, in 1929, where he had been sentenced to serve ten years for burglary; was arrested again in 1930 on a charge of auto larceny and safe blowing and placed in the Kansas State Penitentiary in the same year.

Although Freddie cleverly negotiated a release from prison shortly after meeting Karpis, he kept in close contact with "Alvin" and arranged for their meeting when Karpis' time would be up. It was not long before Karpis did walk out of the pen a free man and set out to meet Fred Barker in Tulsa. There he boastfully confided to Fred, "I got out of there easily. They put me to work in the coal mines. In there you know you're allowed good time for the coal you mine over a certain amount. Well, a lot of my pals were in on life stretches. They didn't mind making a few dollars. I agreed to pay them retail price on all the extra coal they'd mine for me. I turned all this in on my account and got good time for it. Later I paid every convict who'd helped me."

June, 1931, found both Fred and Karpis in the hands of the

law again—charged with the theft of some jewelry in the Barkers' home town, Tulsa. After both escaped serving sentences by making restitution for the theft, they proceeded on to Thayer, Missouri, where "Ma" and Dunlop were living in his cottage.

There were warm greetings and happy tears when "Ma" beheld her favorite son again. She gave instant approval to his excellent choice of companion. With flushed cheeks and sparkling eyes, she proudly brought forward her latest acquisition, Dunlop. Freddie, eyes narrowed, scrutinized the bland features, carefully listened intently to "Ma's" eulogy on his accomplishments and nodded his head. "It's okay. He can stay." Arthur Dunlop automatically rose in prestige and became one of the family while Alvin Karpis moved in as another of "Ma's" foster sons.

For several months life in the Barker household proceeded smoothly enough. The personalities of Freddie and Karpis blended well together and they succeeded in carrying through several profitable undertakings.

MURDER IN MISSOURI

A robbery in West Plains, Missouri, on December 18, 1931, however, was to send them scurrying again for cover. Fred Barker and Alvin Karpis had held up a store, using a 1931 DeSota car for their getaway. On the following day, the West Plains Sheriff, recognizing the car which was parked in a garage, approached the occupants for questioning. As he walked innocently toward them, Fred and Karpis opened fire. The man fell mortally wounded. Later when the police received a tip-off and raided the cottage at Thayer, they found only evidence of the hurried departure of its suspicious occupants.

But the killers were known. They were positively identified as Fred Barker and Alvin Karpis.

The underworld opened its arms and greeted the fugitive band warmly when they fled. First stop was the home of Herbert Farmer in Joplin, Missouri. Farmer, a close friend of the Barker family for years and an accomplished veteran of crime who had given Fred many valuable underworld tips during his boyhood, received them royally and offered his advice, "Your best bet is St. Paul."

Harry Sawyer, great underworld power in St. Paul who was convicted for participating in the Bremer kidnapping with the Barker-Karpis gang, and received a sentence of life imprisonment.

Wires hummed between Joplin and St. Paul as Farmer prepared the way. "Hello, Harry? Yeah. Can you rent a house right away? Friends of mine. They're okay. Right...." And so the nucleus of the Barker-Karpis gang—"Ma," Dunlop, Fred, and Alvin Karpis descended on St. Paul and made the acquaintance of the kingpin and fixer for the St. Paul underworld, Harry Sawyer. With the assurance of his powerful protection, they took up residence in an unpretentious little house in West St. Paul.

However, nerves tightened and tempers flared in a short while, for the fugitives were being sought by various state law-enforcement authorities and consequently were compelled to remain in hiding during the day. At night they would emerge cautiously, carrying a violin case which concealed a sawed-off machine gun.

On April 25, 1932, the landlady's son noticed the photographs of Fred Barker and Alvin Karpis in a detective magazine, indicating they were wanted for the murder of the West Plains Sheriff. He notified the police immediately. However, Harry Sawyer's powerful underground had contacts in the police department and before official police action could be taken, a henchman of Sawyer's was relaying the news to the Barker household. "Somebody's tipped off the police. Harry says you'd better scram fast!"

The flight was on again. But this time only "Ma," Fred Barker and Alvin Karpis travelled together. Dunlop had been dispensed with. His body, stripped of clothing and riddled with bullets fired at close range, was discovered the next morning on the shores of Lake Freasted near Webster, Wisconsin. A blood-soaked woman's glove lay close by. "Ma" and the boys had held court and decided that Dunlop must have been the "squealer."

FORMATION OF THE BARKER-KARPIS GANG

Kansas City, Missouri, was the next "hole" for the fugitives to take cover in, lick their wounds, and rally their forces. "Ma," pompous in costly silks and trailing furs, majestically descended on an exclusive residential district, the Country Club Plaza. She leased an apartment for her sons who were in the insurance business, and herself, and proceeded to take up housekeeping.

Recruits, battle-scarred veterans of the underworld, quickly joined ranks with "Ma" and the boys. There was Francis Keating and Thomas Holden, "hot" convicts, recently escaped from the Federal Penitentiary at Leavenworth and wanted by the FBI; Harvey Bailey, nationally known bank robber; Larry de Vol, an old pal of Karpis; and Bernard Phillips, retired policeman turned robber.

After days of planning, organizing, and preparation, the re-enforced gang descended en masse on a bank in Fort Scott, Kansas, June 17, 1932. While Fred, Karpis, and the boys were looting the bank, "Ma" was at home hysterically weeping, fearful that her Freddie might get injured. When they triumphantly returned that evening laden with the spoils, "Ma" brightened up immediately and proceeded to split the wealth among her dear, dear boys.

On the same evening, Freddie met by pre-arrangement Jess Doyle, a former classmate from the Kansas State Pen, who had just been released that day. After joyfully greeting his convict pal, Freddie pulled a thick wad of bills out of his pocket and pressed them into Doyle's hand. "Just a little somethin' to help you get some new clothes and stuff. Come on home with me. Ma's throwin' a party tonight to celebrate a job we pulled today."

They welcomed Jess Doyle warmly and another hardened recruit was added to the swiftly growing band.

On July 5, 1932, "Mrs. A. F. Hunter and sons" changed residence just as a safety measure and moved into another apartment in Kansas City. For a few days Fred and Karpis enjoyed the homelike atmosphere which "Ma" craftily endeavored to make to fool the neighbors.

But this domestic tranquility was abruptly disturbed on July 7, 1932. FBI Agents on the trail of fugitives Keating and Holden had picked up both of them with Harvey Bailey playing golf on the Old Mission Golf Course at 5:00 in the afternoon. Bernard Phillips, the fourth member of the party, had witnessed the apprehension. Unseen by the Agents, he rushed home to break the news. There was a stunned silence and then Karpis rapped out curt orders. "We've got to move fast. Fred, get the car ready. Ma, start packing...." By 5:30, the apartment was deserted and the Barker-Karpis gang had disappeared into the night.

The gang could afford several hide-outs now. They chose their old stomping grounds, St. Paul, and a summer cottage on White Bear Lake, Minnesota. Flushed with ready money and confident of their power, they relaxed vigilance and indulged in riotous nightlife—drinking, gambling, making love. Their hangouts were a saloon run by their profiteering pal, Harry Sawyer, and a night club operated by John Peifer.

All except "Ma." Cagey, cautious, and overwhelmingly jealous of her boys' "women," she ranted by the hour at their foolishness and tried to break up the friendships. "Drinking is the tool of the devil. Loose tongues will put you behind bars. Those women will be your downfall." But Fred and the boys were not to be deterred. "Ma's" ranting was to no avail. A few expensive gifts, however, for "Ma" as compensation for the boys' mischievousness finally restored domestic bliss.

Although the gang could do nothing to aid their former colleagues, Keating and Holden who were returned to Leavenworth by the FBI, they did engage a criminal lawyer, J. Earl Smith, to defend Harvey Bailey at his trial for the Fort Scott bank robbery in which they had all participated. The combination, however, of Bailey's reputation as a bank robber and the fact that FBI Agents found a liberty bond from the Fort Scott bank on his person at the time of apprehension convinced the jury of his guilt and Harvey Bailey was convicted. The morning after the verdict was reached, August 13, 1932, Bailey's attorney received a mysterious telephone call from Fred Barker to meet him in Tulsa. His bullet-riddled body was discovered the following day on a golf course in Tulsa. "Ma," indignant that the lawyer had failed to secure freedom for one of her boys, had offered him to be "put on the spot." The boys had complied with "Ma's" request willingly.

Additional recruits in the form of Earl Christman, a confidence man and fugitive from the Indiana State Penitentiary, and Helen Ferguson, his moll, augmented the gang at this time. Frank Nash, notorious bank robber and fugitive from Leavenworth, also became a temporary associate.

The gang struck again on July 26, 1932, staging a daring daylight robbery of the Cloud County Bank at Concordia, Kansas. It was a profitable undertaking; the spoils amounted to $240,000.00 in bonds and plenty of cold cash.

"DOC" BARKER COMES HOME

After the gang had returned to the hideout at White Bear Lake and the money had been split, Barker had another thought. Why not attempt to get Arthur out of the Oklahoma State Penitentiary and Lloyd out of Leavenworth? Three sons could make more money than one. She spoke to Freddie. The diminutive five-foot-four outlaw agreed. It was a good idea.

The word went out. Cold cash exchanged hands. Jack Glynn, a former Chief of Police and go-between for convicts and their friends, set to work. Consequently, on September 10, 1932, Arthur "Doc" Barker was released from the Penitentiary. Efforts to secure Lloyd's release, however, failed. Leavenworth could not be tampered with.

The Barker-Karpis gang had a happy reunion when "Doc" joined them in St. Paul. "Ma" was beside herself with joy. She now had two sons to take care of—and two sons to "provide" for her. She enthusiastically plunged into bigger and better plans for the future— jobs which would net thousands of dollars; maybe, in time, millions.

Meanwhile, "Doc" expressed a desire to see his boyhood companion and fellow murderer, convicted with him for the slaying of the night watchman years previously, Volney Davis, who was still incarcerated in the Oklahoma State Penitentiary.

Money and underworld power pulled strings again and on November 3, 1932, Volney Davis set out from prison on a two-years' leave of absence and joined the gang in St. Paul.

Top: William Weaver, member of the Barker-Karpis gang, who received a sentence of life imprisonment for his participation in the Bremer kidnapping.

Bottom: William Weaver's paramour, Myrtle Eaton, who was apprehended with Weaver by Special Agents in Allendale, Florida, where they were running a chicken farm.

Although the citizens of the twin cities and vicinities had up to this time been fairly secure from the depredations of the gang, their safety was short-lived. On December 16, 1932, the Third Northwestern Bank of Minneapolis was robbed. Two police officers and a civilian bystander were killed by a stream of machine gun bullets when they got in the way of the fleeing bandits. The money was divided among Karpis, Fred, "Doc," Larry De Vol, William Weaver, Verne Miller and Jess Doyle.

Five days later Larry De Vol was arrested in his apartment. Sixteen to seventeen thousand dollars of the loot from the Third Northwestern Bank was in his possession.

The gang let him take the "rap" for the robbery and the murders while they hastily departed for Reno, Nevada, where "Ma" Barker, Volney Davis, Earl Christman and Helen Ferguson were waiting. De Vol pleaded guilty to a charge of murder and was sentenced to life imprisonment in the Minnesota State Penitentiary.

PRAIRIE BURIAL AT MIDNIGHT

When the heat cooled off a bit, the desperados headed back to St. Paul where they were joined by a friend of Harry Sawyer's, Eddie Green, an accomplished bank robber. News of a possible police raid on their apartment sent them scurrying to Chicago, Illinois. Here Louis Stacci, underworld power in Chicago, offered temporary haven while they laid plans for their next job, the robbery of a bank at Fairbury, Nebraska.

On April 4, 1933, the gang struck at Fairbury. The robbery was carried off successfully but Earl Christman was severely injured in the getaway attempt. Fred, "Doc," and Karpis rushed the dying man to the home of Verne Miller, their old consort and professional killer. An underworld physician was summoned but Christman failed to respond to the treatment and died.

Under cover of darkness that night, the gang conducted its own burial service, far enough away from the vicinity so that the police could never find the corpse. When the gangster's mother heard of his death and made frantic pleas to learn the location of her son's grave, the gang gravely considered the request. It was steely-eyed Karpis who vetoed it saying, "If she goes and digs up that stiff the cops may hear about it. They may find a clue that would start them after us." The Barker-Karpis gang sent its regrets to Earl Christman's mother.

Mrs. C. P. Harmon, paramour of Fred Barker, was committed to a State Hospital for mental disorders after she broke off her association with the gang.

Shortly, after the Fairbury incident, attractive Paula Harmon, widow of a notorious bank robber, Charles Harmon, joined Fred Barker as his moll and the couple took up residence in St. Paul under the name of Mr. and Mrs. J. Stanley Smith. "Ma" and the other members of the gang established themselves in cottages at Bald Eagle Lake, Minnesota.

It was here that "Ma" broke the news to her brood. From now on bank robbery was beneath their dignity. They were going to go after bigger game. Their new *modus operandi*—kidnapping.

THE HAMM KIDNAPPING

As their *coup de main* the gang decided to "snatch" William A. Hamm, Jr., wealthy St. Paul beer brewer. Accordingly, on June 15, 1933, the luckless victim was seized and transported to Bensenville, Illinois. Ransom negotiations proceeded swiftly and efficiently in the capable hands of shady citizens of the underworld acting as intermediaries between the frantic family and the kidnappers. Four days later, June 19, 1933, Hamm, alive and unharmed, was released and the coffers of the Barker-Karpis gang overflowed with crisp, green currency—$100,000 worth. "Ma" Barker's new business venture had turned out to be quite profitable.

Top: Fred Goetz, former collegiate football player and member of the Barker-Karpis gang was murdered by his associates. Irene Dorsey, his paramour, was located in an insane asylum.

Bottom: Bryan Bolton, member of the Barker-Karpis gang, was apprehended by Special Agents in Chicago on January 8, 1935.

Settling temporarily in Chicago while the "heat was on" in St. Paul, the gang carefully and methodically made plans for the future. New recruits, including Fred Goetz, one-time college football player and former associate of the Al Capone syndicate; Bryan Bolton, tubercular stooge of Fred Goetz; and Harry Campbell, former childhood pal of the Barkers and associate of Glen Leroy Wright, notorious Oklahoma outlaw, joined the ranks and offered their services and experiences.

Harry Campbell, member of the Barker-Karpis gang and murderer, received a sentence of life imprisonment for his participation in the Bremer kidnapping case.

Drunk with their continued successes, the gang embarked on a rampage of crime in the Midwest. A payroll robbery of the Stockyards National Bank at South St. Paul on August 1933, netted the outlaws $30,000.00. In the getaway attempt their bullets riddled two police officers—killing one and permanently maiming the other. Less than a month later—a Chicago policeman was machine-gunned to death, another innocent victim of the gang.

THE BREMER KIDNAPPING

The latter part of December, 1933, found the gang firmly ensconced once more in their most profitable "theater of operations"—the Twin Cities, and energetically laying plans for their next "snatch." This time the victim was to be Edward George Bremer, 36-year-old scion from one of the wealthiest and most prominent families in St. Paul and president of the Commercial State Bank.

On January 17, 1934, the gang successfully kidnapped the youthful magnate as he was driving to the Bank after leaving his nine-year-old daughter off at school. As Bremer paused for a stop sign, masked men brandishing pistols pulled open the front doors of his Lincoln sedan. Forcing him to move out from under the wheel, they clubbed him with a blunt instrument, then pushed the body to the floor of the car with his head under the instrument board. Taped goggles were placed over his eyes.

While Karpis, "Doc", Harry Campbell and William Weaver were transporting the victim to their hideout at Bensenville, Illinois, other members of the gang were beginning ransom negotiations.

Walter Magee, close friend of the Bremer family, was contacted and issued instructions on the amount of ransom desired and the payment thereof. For three long weeks Bremer was imprisoned in the Illinois farm house while the gang carried on negotiations with his anxious family. But this time, hovering silently, watchful in the background, was the nemesis of the underworld, the FBI.

Aware through the underworld grapevine of the G-Men's silent interest in the case, the gang nervously stalled for time in their negotiations while they hastily checked and rechecked their plans for payment of the ransom. There must be no "slip-up"; no evidence carelessly left behind to feed the insatiable curiosity of the FBI. There were already too many casualties in the front lines of the underworld—all credited to the persevering G-Men. Daily, familiar faces were plastered on the front pages of the press and bold black type announced their death or capture by Hoover's Agents. The Barker-Karpis gang determined that this would not happen to them. Bremer was kept blindfolded the greater part of his imprisonment; "Doc" Barker used a Mexican accent when talking to the victim to conceal his southern drawl; elaborate, fool-proof preparations for the pay-off were drawn up.

On the evening of February 6, 1934, Walter Magee in compliance with the kidnapper's instructions found a 1933 Chevrolet coupe bearing Shell Oil Company signs on each door at a designated street corner in St. Paul. In the left front pocket of the coupe, he found the keys to the car and a note.

"Go to Farmington, Minnesota. The Rochester bus will arrive there at 9:15 P.M. and leave at 9:25 P.M.. Follow one hundred yards in back of this bus when it leaves Farmington until you come to four red lights on the left of the road; turn on the first road to the left and proceed at fifteen miles per hour until you see five flashes of lights; then stop and deposit packages of money on right hand side of road. Leave the note; get in car and go straight ahead."

The intermediary followed directions to the letter and deposited the ransom, $200,000.00 in five and ten-dollar bills, on the side of the road and drove on. The next evening, the victim, weak from nervous exhaustion, was released on a lonely street in the suburbs of Rochester, Minnesota.

IN THE FBI SPOTLIGHT

With the news of Bremer's safe release, the FBI set smoothly into action its mighty investigative machine. Under the leadership of J. Edgar Hoover, Special Agents turned grimly to the task of determining the identity of the kidnappers. No lead or clue was too small for consideration. Bremer's story of the kidnapping ride, his imprisonment in what seemed to him to be a farm house, the treatment of his kidnappers, the sound of their voices, distinguishing characteristics of the room in which he was confined, were all duly recorded.

Three days after Bremer's release, February 10, 1934, Special Agents uncovered the first hint of the identity of the kidnappers. A gasoline can, used by the gang to refill their tank when returning the victim to Minnesota, was found near Portage, Wisconsin. Positively identified by Bremer, the evidence was rushed to the FBI Laboratory in Washington. Agents waited breathlessly for the Laboratory's report.

When it came, they swung into action. There had been two latent prints on the can: fingerprints positively identified by technicians as being those of Arthur "Doc" Barker. Teletypes flooded the country to all SAC's: "Pick up the Barker-Karpis gang ... Wanted for kidnapping of Edward George Bremer ... Description as follows ... Urgent ... "

The FBI for the first time had federal jurisdiction to seek the apprehension of the notorious gang. The period of watchful waiting was over.

THE BEGINNING OF THE END

With the breath of the G-Men hot on their backs, the Barker-Karpis gang momentarily lost their arrogance and fled to Chicago. Splitting up into smaller groups, they barricaded themselves in apartments furnished by their underworld contacts.

Dr. Joseph P. Moran, underworld physician, who operated on the fingers and faces of Karpis, Fred and "Doc" Barker, Volney Davis and Harry Campbell, was murdered by the gang. According to underworld rumor his body was placed in a barrel of wet cement and thrown in Lake Erie.

On March 10, 1934, one of Chicago's underworld "medicos," Dr. Moran, operated on the fingers and faces of Fred Barker and Alvin Karpis in an unsuccessful attempt to alter their fingerprints and facial characteristics.

This picture shows the results of the facial operation which Dr. Moran had performed in an attempt to disguise Karpis' appearance.

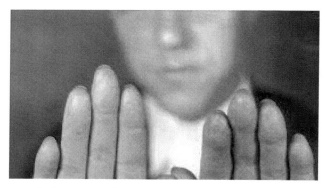

This photograph shows the fingertips of Alvin Karpis after Dr. Moran had operated on them in an unsuccessful attempt to obliterate his fingerprints. Karpis was sentenced to life imprisonment in the United States penitentiary at Alcatraz.

On March 20, 1934, Comrade Fred Goetz lost favor with the gang and was murdered. In an effort to prevent identification several shotgun blasts were fired in his face. Agents, however, identified the murdered gangster by his fingerprints. The FBI concentrated on a search for Goetz's paramour, Irene Dorsey. She was found in a mental ward of a hospital. Her mind had broken down under the strain of her association with the mob. William

Harrison, powerful contact for the gang and court "jester," in an unguarded moment talked too much with acquaintances of the gang. Lured by his companions to an abandoned barn in the vicinity of Ontarioville, Illinois, he was shot to death, his body soaked in gasoline and the barn set on fire.

On April 22, 1934, John Dillinger and his mobsters, fleeing from capture by FBI Agents, sought temporary refuge with the gang and were warmly welcomed. After performing similar unsuccessful facial and finger operations on "Doc" Barker, Volney Davis and Harry Campbell, Dr. Moran was knocked unconscious by the gang. According to underworld rumor his body was placed in a barrel of wet cement and thrown in Lake Erie.

Left: William Harrison, member of the Barker-Karpis gang who was murdered by the gang because he talked too much. Center: Russell Gibson, member of the Barker-Karpis gang who was killed by Special Agents while resisting arrest in Chicago on January 8, 1935.

Right: Oliver Berg, who received a sentence of life imprisonment for his participation in the Bremer kidnapping case.

Meanwhile, the FBI was diligently following down every clue, constructing an air-tight web of evidence which would permanently ensnare the vicious gangsters on their apprehension.

Other Agents under the personal direction of J. Edgar Hoover were ferreting out the mobsters and their contacts one by one. "Boss" McLaughlin, a political "ward heeler" and ex-Illinois State legislator, was picked up, charged with exchanging the ransom money for the gang. An escaped inmate of the Illinois State Penitentiary and one of the few surviving members of the notorious "Bugs" Moran mob, Oliver A. Berg, was apprehended at the home of his sister in Chicago, charged with furnishing the ransom money to McLaughlin.

The net was growing tighter. "Ma" Barker and Fred fled to Florida; Alvin Karpis and his woman, Dolores Delaney, to Cuba. "Doc" Barker, his moll, Mildred Kuhlman, Russell Gibson and Bryan Bolton remained in Chicago.

On the night of January 8, 1935, "Doc" Barker's Chicago apartment was surrounded by Special Agents. At 6:30 P.M., "Doc" and Mildred Kuhlman stepped out into the street. They were surrounded. "Doc" surrendered without resistance. On the same evening the apartment occupied by Russell Gibson, his wife, Bryan Bolton and the ex-wife of William Harrison, was raided.

Ignoring the pleas of his wife to surrender, Russell Gibson chose to fight it out. His one shot at a Special Agent missed its mark but the Agent's returning fire punctured his bulletproof vest and mortally wounded him. He died a few hours later in a Chicago hospital with a curse on his lips for all law enforcement officers.

Arthur "Doc" Barker was given a sentence of life imprisonment in the United States Penitentiary, Alcatraz Island, for his participation in the Bremer kidnapping, and was killed on January 19, 1939, in an attempt to escape from Alcatraz.

Special Agents on searching "Doc" Barker's apartment found an invaluable clue—a map, on which a circle had been drawn around the town of Ocala, Florida, near Lake Weir. This confirmed confidential reports received that "Ma" and Fred Barker were hiding out in Florida near a lake.

The men of the FBI readied preparations to descend on Lake Weir.

The cottage at Lake Weir in which "Ma" and Fred Barker were killed
while resisting arrest.

DEATH AT LAKE WEIR

It was 5:30 A.M., January 16, 1935. A caravan of black sedans
drove slowly along Highway 41 turning off on a dirt road. Lake
Weir, shrouded in early morning mist, lay straight ahead. A corps
of grave-faced men, bearing high-powered rifles, machine guns,
tear gas bombs, poured out of the parked cars and proceeded
along the road to the lake on foot. Their destination was a little
white cottage, standing aristocratically apart from its neighbors
on a mossy slope.

Its occupants slumbered soundly on as the men approached it
and melted into the surrounding shrubbery.

The signal was given. A voice spoke resonantly...."Kate Barker,
Fred Barker. This is the FBI. You are surrounded. Come out one at
a time with your hands up....."

There was a sudden tense silence. FBI Agents cocked their
guns in readiness. Minutes passed. Movements were heard inside
the cottage. The command was repeated again.

"Ma" and Fred Barker maintained a stony silence.

An Agent shouted. "Unless you come out, we'll use tear gas."
This time there was an answer.

"Ma's" voice bellowed triumphantly as she sent a stream of lead
pouring out through an upstairs window. "All right, go ahead."

The battle began as the first rays of the morning sun spread fan-like across the leaden sky. Tear gas bombs were hurled into the bullet smashed windows. The Barkers answered with bursts of machine gun fire—from the second floor and from the first floor near the entrance to the cottage.

Agents partially concealed behind nearby trees systematically poured lead into every portion of the frame shelter.

"Ma" Barker retaliated savagely, spraying the foliage with deadly accuracy.

The exchange of gunfire raged for several hours. Then, suddenly, silence within the cottage.

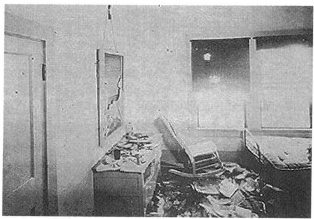

The bedroom in which "Ma" and Fred Barker were found dead.

Cautiously, Agents kicked opened the flimsy door. A winding trail of blood led them upstairs to a bullet-shattered bedroom. There they found two figures slumped on the wooden floor—Fred Barker, lying in the middle of the room, face down, with a .45 automatic under him and a machine gun with a 50 shot drum under his left hand—close by, "Ma" Barker, lying on her back, with a machine gun and hundred shot drum beside her lifeless body. The barrel was still smoking.

True to the traditions of gangsterism, they had died defying their sworn enemy—the law.

Special Agents retrieved a small arsenal on searching the cottage.

Gangdom, however, deserted "Ma" and Fred Barker in death. For eight months their bodies remained unburied. On October 1, 1935, they were placed to rest in an unknown countryside graveyard, choked with undergrowth and weeds, known as the Williams Cemetery, Oklahoma. Their graves were dug next to the remains of "Ma's" oldest son, Herman Barker.

"CREEPY" KARPIS IN FLIGHT

Alvin Karpis, called "Old Creepy" by his paramour because of his cold stare and precision in carrying out his crimes, found it increasingly more and more difficult after the deaths of "Ma" and Fred Barker to rally his fast depleting forces.

One by one, the FBI was plucking them out of their hiding places. On May 3, 1935, Harry Sawyer was apprehended in Mississippi; on June 1, 1935, Volney Davis was seized in Chicago; on September 1, William Weaver was picked up in Chicago.

Karpis clung desperately to his toppling throne with Harry Campbell, his sole "subject" as the underworld regretfully closed its doors on him. In the eyes of its cautious citizens Alvin Karpis was "too hot."

He fled from Cuba, to New Jersey, to Ohio, to Oklahoma. But always the men of the FBI were close on his trail.

Cornered, the enraged fugitive planned futilely to wage a one-man war against the FBI. He wrote a letter to J. Edgar Hoover advising that he was coming to FBI Headquarters with a "machine gun." Typical of the number one gangster of the day, he seriously considered killing the top FBI officials in the Los Angeles, New York and Chicago Field Offices; thus, as he thought, striking a crippling blow to the forces of his enemy. But each time the killer's cold logical mind came to his rescue and calmed his passionate outbursts.

Alvin Karpis did find temporary refuge, however. This time in gangdom's utopia—Hot Springs, Arkansas. He made friends with the "law"—"greasing the greedy palms" of its Chief of Police, Joseph Wakelin, his obsequious understudy, Herbert Akers, Chief of Detectives, and their satellite, Cecil Brock, Lieutenant in Charge of the Identification Division.

While an FBI wanted notice for Karpis yellowed with age on the Hot Springs city jail door and press releases dealing with the progress of the FBI's manhunt for the killer flooded the city's newspapers, "Creepy" Karpis and his new recruit, 37-year-old ex-convict Fred Hunter, were enjoying the facilities of the open city—its baths, night clubs, houses of ill-repute.

The fugitives made the acquaintance of two of the "ladies of the evening"—and adopted them for their constant companions—Grace Goldstein for Karpis and 21-year-old Connie Morris for Hunter.

The happy foursome spent money lavishly in a mad round of excitement. And what was even more pleasing to Karpis, Wakelin and Akers officially cleared the way for their uninterrupted revelry.

It was a perfect "set up." So ideal that Karpis began to send out appeals through the underworld grapevine for new recruits. Harry Campbell came out of hiding and answered the call enthusiastically. A prison pal of former members of the Barker-Karpis gang, John Brock, proceeded to negotiate for admittance. Sam Coker, former boyhood friend of the Barkers, was contacted on his release from the Oklahoma State Penitentiary and persuaded to become one of the chosen few.

Re-enforced and revengeful, Alvin Karpis plunged recklessly

back into his criminal activities. On November 7, 1935, an Erie Train at Garretsville, Ohio, en route from Detroit to Pittsburgh, was held up by bandits armed with machine guns and shotguns. Thirty-four thousand dollars in currency and several thousand dollars in securities composed the haul.

Discarding the old-fashioned method of making a getaway in a fast, high-powered car, the bandits piled into an airplane piloted by a friend and flew back to their retreat, gracious Hot Springs.

After the spoils had been split and Campbell accompanied by Coker returned to Toledo, Ohio, Karpis and Fred Hunter resumed their pleasurable activities in Hot Springs. But this time there was a slight tinge of frost in the air.

The "law" was beginning to feel the growing tension of the city's citizens as they recognized Alvin Karpis in their midst. Rumors began to trickle out of Hot Springs. The "law" tried to smother them, to laugh them off. But they persisted, grew stronger. Five thousand dollars reward for information leading to the apprehension of Alvin Karpis could not be dismissed so easily—a handsome reward for just putting the finger on Karpis. It would "look good," too, helping the FBI track down such a dangerous fugitive....

But Alvin Karpis' ears were pressed to the ground, too. Two days before the Hot Springs Chief of Police reported to the FBI that a man resembling Karpis was seen in his territory, the wily fugitive fled. With him were Fred Hunter, Connie Morris and Grace Goldstein. Their destination was New Orleans.

On receiving the report from Wakelin, Special Agents combed the Hot Springs area thoroughly, uncovering with uncanny precision the corrupt practices of the existing police force. The scandal grew in proportion as the FBI tenaciously probed deeper. Aroused citizens confided that they had seen the Chief of Police and his companions in the company of Alvin Karpis. An old FBI wanted notice was found prominently displayed on the jail door.

As a result of the FBI's investigation, which blew the lid off their scheming racket, the Hot Springs police force temporarily resigned to await federal trial on a charge of violating the Federal Harboring Statute.

Several months later, Joseph Wakelin, Herbert Akers and Cecil Brock faced a federal judge and received their sentences. Two years' imprisonment in a federal penitentiary for each of them.

Meanwhile, exhaustive investigation by the indefatigable men of the FBI ferreted out the fugitive's new hiding place.

Under the leadership of Director Hoover, a small band of Special Agents closed in on the desperate fugitive.

The apartment building at 3343 Canal Street, New Orleans, Louisiana, last hide out of Alvin Karpis and Fred Hunter.

THE LAST STAND

The date was May 1, 1936. New Orleans, city of fable and frivolity, was stirring lazily after its afternoon siesta. The shadows of the sun fell on the ancient sun dial, marking the time as 5:30 P.M..

The exclusive apartment building at 3343 Canal Street stood quietly in repose, flanked on all sides by squares of white pavement and luxurious shrubbery. A parked Plymouth coupe sat idly before its dignified facade.

Suddenly, the scrolled iron door of the building was pushed open. Two men stepped out.

Agents concealed in the surrounding shrubbery recognized the men as Alvin Karpis and Fred Hunter.

The late sun's rays flickered hesitatingly over Karpis' inscrutable countenance as he and his companion stepped briskly down the five steps to the sidewalk.

J. Edgar Hoover gave the signal to his men. Silently, they began to slip out from their hiding places. Up and down the quiet street parked cars began to warm their motors imperceptibly and to slide easily down the wide avenue.

The two men reached the coupe. Hunter reached into his pocket for the key. Guns drawn, the men of the FBI approached. Suddenly, a child's happy cry split the silence. A small boy on a red scooter sped down the walk past the men who were now entering the coupe.

Agents froze in their tracks. The child would be caught in the cross-fire if Karpis began shooting. They waited breathlessly until he had scooted safely by.

By this time the coupe's motor was turning over. The car gathered momentum and began to pull away from the curb.

Instantly, the cruising cars roared into action, surrounding the fugitive's car on all sides. The door to the coupe was pulled open. Alvin Karpis looked up to see the hand of his hated adversary, Hoover, himself, tap his arm. He heard him say, "Alvin Karpis ... G-Men ... You're under arrest."

The fugitive turned ashen white. His cold stare melted under the penetrating glance of the stern-eyed men surrounding him.

Running his tongue over suddenly dry lips, he tremblingly acknowledged his capture. The saga of "Creepy" Karpis was through.

Sidearms and rifles found in Alvin Karpis' car on his apprehension.

EPILOGUE TO CRIME

With the capture of Harry Campbell and Sam Coker six days later in Toledo, Ohio, the Barker-Karpis gang was completely eradicated.

Twenty-five members of the gang were convicted in connection with the abduction of Edward George Bremer. Sentences varied— six life imprisonments; one hundred years and one day; four thousand dollar fines; three persons killed while resisting arrest and three murdered by fellow members.

With the passing years a gradual metamorphosis occurred in the mind of Alvin Karpis at Alcatraz. From the lonely solitude of his cell he penned a strange message to someone he loved:

"I suppose by now you realize that all that glitters is not gold.... When you are released from prison, stay on the straight and narrow path.... You will think that rather strange coming from me, but I should know."

There are over one hundred and fifty volumes composing the mammoth file on the Barker-Karpis gang—volumes which trace the criminals' vain attempt to reap wealth, power and happiness by brute force.

The epilogue to this way of life is always the same—Fool's gold ... stay on the straight and narrow ... I learned too late....

Wanted

John Herbert Dillinger

Twelve years ago the newspapers of America were recording the career of John Dillinger in bold, black headlines.

Over breakfast tables and lunch counters, in smoky poolrooms and dimly-lit saloons, the latest choice morsels of the desperado's activities were avidly discussed. Sob sisters painted romantic pictures of the misguided youth and his red-headed sweetheart, Evelyn Frechette. Thousands of women sighed at the adventures of the dangerous duo and would gladly have exchanged places with Evelyn for just "one day in the sun." American youth chewed gum, adopted the Hollywood version of the underworld argot, and began to shift their adolescent hero-worship from "wild-western movie cowboys" to the notorious gun-men of the day—John Dillinger, "Baby Face" Nelson, Homer Van Meter, John Chase, Tommy Carroll, John Hamilton. The pulse of the nation, stimulated by the shallow glamour and robust sensualities of these public enemies, quickened perceptibly and almost over night, public opinion swayed to an alarming admiration for the cleverness of the Dillinger mob.

Momentarily forgotten was the brutal, mass murder of four law enforcement officers and their cringing prisoner, Frank Nash, at the Union Railway Station in Kansas City in June, 1933, by the vicious trio, Verne Miller, "Pretty Boy" Floyd and Adam Richetti. Forgotten also were the innumerable, cold-blooded killings of innocent citizens and law enforcement officers who inadvertently stepped in the way of ruthless gangsters in the past.

But the Federal Bureau of Investigation had not forgotten. It knew the potential deadliness of these "new comers" on crime's horizon. It recognized a familiar pattern in the depredations of the Dillinger mob for it was at that time seeking the apprehension of their contemporaries, the "Barker-Karpis" gang.

Special Agents made quiet preparations to take up one of the most dangerous manhunts of the day. They knew that eventually John Dillinger's crime career would embrace federal violations which would bring him within FBI investigative jurisdiction.

For almost a year, the FBI waited patiently while the Dillinger mob ran through the gamut of crime without committing a Federal offense....

Early photograph of 30-year-old John Dillinger after he was released on parole from the Indiana State Prison. In this picture Dillinger's cleft chin and mole between the eyebrows may be easily seen.

BACKGROUND ON JOHN DILLINGER

John Dillinger, 20-year-old Indiana farm boy, was shut up in the Indiana State Prison, charged with robbing and beating his father's friend, the neighborhood grocer, in September of 1924.

Nine years later, bitter, surly, intent on revenge, he emerged from prison on parole. He determined to get even with society.

Within four months after his release, he was well on the way. He had robbed eight banks successfully and was richer by over $100,000.

Cocky and confident of his unfailing luck, he smuggled guns and a getaway chart over the walls of the Indiana prison to his former cronies. However, when the convicts made their escape on September 26, 1933, Dillinger was not on hand to greet them. He had been captured by the Ohio police for bank robbery and placed in the County Jail at Lima, Ohio.

Undaunted by the news, three of the convicts, Harry Pierpont, Russell Clark and Charles Makley, decided to return John's favor to them and rescue him from the law.

On the night of October 12, 1933, they descended on Sheriff Sarber's office at Lima, shot the Sheriff and, using the butt of a pistol, beat him into unconsciousness. After freeing Dillinger, they fled.

John Hamilton, one of ten convicts who escaped from the Indiana State Prison on September 26, 1933. After joining the Dillinger gang, he embarked on a series of bank robberies throughout the Midwest. During the flight from the Bohemia Inn raid, he was mortally wounded and died ten days later. Hamilton was known as "Red" Hamilton to his gangster buddies after he dyed his hair red to escape detection by the FBI.

Dangerous living came easily to Dillinger and his colleagues as they embarked on a pillage of the midwest. Joined by John Hamilton, a fellow escapee from the Indiana Prison, they forced their way into two Indiana police departments, seizing machine guns, rifles, revolvers, bullet-proof vests and a load of ammunition.

Continuing their forced march, they swooped down on the Greencastle, Indiana bank. Greedy hands divided the $74,000 in loot. On November 20, Dillinger, Makley, Hamilton and Pierpont robbed the American Bank & Trust Co. at Racine and escaped with $28,000.

Arrogantly bearing their weapons of death, they descended on Chicago. Here, the "Big Business of Crime," after reviewing their background and qualifications meticulously, set the official seal of approval on them. The Dillinger mob met the big shots of underworld society—the Barker boys and their "Ma", "Old Creepy" Karpis, Eddie Green and scores of ambitious criminal proteges.

Left: The 33-year-old member of the original Dillinger gang, Russell Clark, who escaped from the Indiana State Prison in September, 1933, was also convicted for the murder of the sheriff at Lima and received a sentence of life imprisonment.

Center: Charles Makley, after his capture in Tucson on January 25, 1934, with Dillinger, Clark and Pierpoint, was returned to Ohio and convicted for the murder of the Lima, Ohio sheriff, receiving a life sentence. On September 22, 1934, Makley was killed in an attempted escape from prison.

Right: Harry Pierpoint, escaped convict who also participated in the murder of the Lima, Ohio sheriff, received the death sentence. In less than a month after being wounded in the attempted break from prison in which Makley was killed, Pierpoint was executed. The date was October 17, 1934.

Fawning sycophants, living off the gang lord's plentiful supply of blood money, offered their services—casual women, overnight shelter, mutilated fingerprints, a new nose, wigs, hair dyes, legal advice, "tommy" guns, high-powered cards, good liquor.... The fee was staggering but the service was unexcelled and unrivalled.

The gang, however, did not tarry very long in Chicago. John Hamilton's trigger finger had nervously sent a blast of gunfire at a local police detective who had cornered him in a garage. On the officer's death, the "boys" left town to spare their underworld pals any possible inquisition from probing law enforcement officials.

Death was a ready companion as they continued pursuing their criminal careers. It struck again, one month later, January

15, 1934, in East Chicago, Indiana. This time it was John Dillinger who loosed a hail of lead at a policeman. The gang had been in the midst of robbing the First National Bank at East Chicago when the officer intruded. Scooping up two thousand dollars in currency, they set out for Florida to "cool off."

Eveyln Frechette, who was John Dillinger's paramour, received a two-year sentence and a $1,000 fine after she was apprehended by FBI agents on April 9, 1934.

The "women" came along on this trip, too. John Dillinger's paramour, 27-year-old Evelyn Frechette, the wife of a former gangster associate; Harry Pierpont's girl, Mary Kinder, and Russell Clark's woman, Opal Long.

For a few days the tropical climate appeased the excitement-crazed gang but it soon wore off. En masse, they travelled to Tucson, Arizona.

Registering at a hotel under assumed names, they continued their gay round of night-life. A fire at the hotel cut short their celebration. Observing firemen, recognizing the gangsters from their pictures in a detective magazine, notified the Tucson police. Dillinger, Pierpont, Clark and Makley, caught unawares, were arrested promptly. Dillinger, under heavy guard, was whisked off to Crown Point, Indiana, to await trial for the murder of the East Chicago officer. The other three were returned to Ohio and convicted for the murder of the sheriff at Lima, Ohio. Of the original gang, Hamilton, alone, was unapprehended. Severely wounded in the East Chicago bank robbery, he was convalescing in Chicago with Pat Cherrington, his paramour, at the time of the Tucson raid.

THE FBI GOES ON THE TRAIL OF JOHN DILLINGER

The nation breathed a sigh of relief with the news of Dillinger's capture in Tucson. John Dillinger had become just a little too "exciting." The mantle of glamour and intrigue was slipping away. Now he was known as a killer—a man with cold eyes and sneering lips who ruthlessly cut down any obstacle in his path.

On March 3, 1934, John Dillinger escaped again. This time he subdued the Crown Point prison guards by using a wooden gun whittled from a washboard and daubed with shoe polish. The ruse worked and Dillinger, seizing the Sheriff's car, fled from Indiana to Illinois.

On receiving the news of Dillinger's spectacular break, the Federal Bureau of Investigation swept into action. This was the "loophole" they had been waiting for. In stealing the Sheriff's car, John Dillinger had violated the National Motor Vehicle Theft Act. At last this notorious public enemy was within the investigative jurisdiction of the FBI.

Teletypes clacked urgently to all field offices: "Cover all leads seeking apprehension of John Dillinger." FBI Identification Orders, giving the criminal's fingerprints, description, photo, criminal record, found their way into the hands of every law enforcement official in the country. All known relatives, close friends and contacts of Dillinger were placed under surveillance. Inspector Sam Cowley was made directly responsible for the Dillinger investigation....

THE NEW DILLINGER GANG

John Dillinger fled in the Sheriff's car to Chicago. There he sought the "professional services" offered so liberally once before. The underworld was receptive but firm. It could take care of the fugitive but now with the "G-Men" cracking down on him the price would be twice as much. Criminal contacts were not eager to risk their profitable business without some "risk insurance."

Three days later, March 6, 1934, a carload of gangsters descended on the Security National Bank at Sioux Falls, South Dakota. When the smoke from the criminals' guns cleared, $49,500 was missing and Motorcycle Patrolman Hale Keith was found shot.

The FBI picked up the rumor spreading along the underworld grapevine. "John Dillinger has new mob. They pulled off the Sioux Falls job. Their names—'Baby Face' Nelson, Homer Van Meter, Tommy Carroll and Dillinger's old convict buddy, John Hamilton...." Special Agents redoubled their efforts to trace down every lead which might give them an inkling of the desperados' hideouts.

Top: Eddie Green, member of the Barker-Karpis gang, who harbored the Dillinger gang in St. Paul, was killed while resisting arrest by FBI agents.

Bottom: Patricia Cherrington, John Hamilton's paramour, who was taken into custody by agents on June 2, 1934, was sentenced to two years in a federal penitentiary.

Meanwhile, the new Dillinger Gang hastened on to St. Paul. Here they were introduced to the famous underworld host, Harry Sawyer. Sawyer, with the aid of Eddie Green, member of the Barker-Karpis gang, hustled around getting the gang appropriate living accommodations. Green found an apartment one block from his own for Dillinger and Evelyn Frechette. Apartments were also secured for Lester Gillis, alias "Baby Face" Nelson, his wife, Helen Gillis, and their five-year-old son; Tommy Carroll and his paramour, Jean Delaney, the sister of Dolores Delaney, who was the current mistress of Alvin "Old Creepy" Karpis at the time; Homer Van Meter and his woman, Marie Conforti; and John Hamilton and his sweetheart, twice-married Pat Cherrington.

Seven days after the Sioux Falls bank robbery, March 13, 1934, Dillinger and the "boys" swooped down on the First National Bank at Mason City, Iowa. This time the "swag" amounted to over $52,000. But in the ensuing gun battle with local authorities, John Dillinger and Hamilton were injured.

Returning to St. Paul that night, the gang sent out an urgent appeal along the underground route for a doctor to treat their bullet wounds. One of Harry Sawyer's former bootleggers, Pat Reilly, offered to furnish the doctor.

Midnight found the obsequious Reilly ushering John Dillinger and Hamilton into the hallway of the Reilly's family physician. The unsuspecting doctor, roused from sleep, made a cursory examination of the gangsters' wounds, advised them that their injuries were only superficial and treated them accordingly. Standing guard over the doctor's house while his buddies were within was Homer Van Meter with a machine gun concealed under his coat.

DISSENSION IN THE RANKS

A brief vacation from crime soon healed the wounds of the two gangsters. But there was a new tension in the air now. It even permeated the impregnable spirit of John Dillinger. The tension revolved around "Baby Face" Nelson. For the first time, Dillinger came in contact with a man who challenged his authority. The rest of the mob, except Nelson's buddy, John Chase, disliked and feared "Baby Face" intensely. Dillinger found himself sharing the common opinion resenting the mutual conspiracy which the gang always engaged in when splitting a large "take" after pulling off a bank robbery. "Baby Face," unaware that it had been arranged purposely, was always placed in the middle of the room and allowed to count and divide the loot. The rest of the gang sat around facing him. They expected at any time that Nelson might try to shoot them and take the entire amount. He was noted for his insatiable greed and love of blood. Dillinger resolved to break with Nelson after the next profitable job.

The "G" heat, however, prevented further dissension among the gang. It had grown into an intense blaze as the men of the FBI, working day and night, continued their patient, probing investigation. On March 31, 1934, it almost caught up with the mob....

Word had been received the evening of March 30 from the manager of a St. Paul apartment house that the tenants in one of her apartments were acting suspiciously. Immediately, Agents contacted the manager in person. Her story, based largely on generalities, was carefully checked. An all-night surveillance was kept on the apartment house. No suspicious activities, however, were noted. Photographs of numerous criminals were exhibited to the manager. She identified none. Consequently, the next morning, a Special Agent accompanied by a local police officer proceeded to the apartment for a routine questioning of its occupants.

They knocked on the door. Several moments elapsed before the door was pulled open by an attractive, red-haired woman. Her eyes widened with alarm as she stared at them. Before they could speak, she slammed the door shut and pulled the iron latch.

The Agent, sensing the unnatural furtiveness of the strange young woman, raced to the stairs to put in a call for additional men. On the way down, he almost collided with a dapper young man entering the hallway. Suspicious of the stranger's actions, the Agent asked him his business. The young man answered pleasantly that he was a soap salesman. Still not completely satisfied the FBI man began to follow the retreating stranger, who suddenly ducked into a doorway leading to the basement and pulled a gun. Facing the Agent, he snarled. "You asked for it, so I'll give it to you now." Spraying the lobby with bullets, the "soap salesman," alias Homer Van Meter, dashed down the basement stairs and out the back entrance. Unhurt, the Agent rushed to a phone and called the St. Paul office as the chatter of a machine gun from the second floor reached his ears. While additional Agents were en route to the apartment house, Evelyn Frechette and John Dillinger fled through the rear entrance, covering their retreat with murderous machine gun fire. In the exchange of gunfire between the Agent and the fleeing gangster, Dillinger was hit in the leg just above the knee.

AN ATTEMPTED RETREAT

Dillinger's narrow escape on March 31 marked the beginning of the end for the notorious fugitive. Former contacts, harborers, and friends, began to attempt disappearing acts—only to be rooted out by the patiently, probing FBI. Eddie Green was the first. Cornered by the "G-Men" in a St. Paul apartment on April 3, he had chosen to fight rather than surrender. He died from the gunshot wounds a week later. Next located was the doctor who had treated the flesh wound in Dillinger's leg after his escape from the St. Paul apartment. He proved to be Dr. Clayton E. May, a Minneapolis physician, whose chief practice consisted in performing illegal operations. The trail led to the home of Dr. May's practical nurse. FBI Agents discovered that Dillinger and Evelyn Frechette had remained in hiding there while the fugitive's leg was being treated.

The day after the shooting of Eddie Green, Dillinger and Evelyn Frechette fled to Mooresville, Indiana, with the FBI following close behind them. Here, Dillinger's family harbored the desperate couple. Several days later they moved on to Chicago. But the men of the FBI were waiting there, too. Dillinger got away but his stormy mistress was not so fortunate. One month later, she faced a Federal judge and was given two years in the Federal penitentiary and fined $1,000 for harboring John Dillinger. Dr. May was also found guilty at this time and received a similar sentence. The pertinacious probing of the FBI was beginning to pay off.

Fully realizing the difficulty of trying to apprehend a man protected on all sides by unscrupulous members of the crime empire, FBI Agents bore down on their drive to locate every contact and "fixer" connected with the gang. The cooperation of all local law enforcement agencies was solicited. They were asked to immediately report any suspicious activities in their districts to the federal authorities. Citizens were warned to be on the alert for a man with a mole between his eyebrows and a prominent cleft in his chin. Agents were posted in crime-infested Chicago, St. Paul, Minneapolis, Reno ... the trail often led from a word dropped carelessly by a cheap thug in a Chicago poolroom, to an exclusive St. Paul night club, on to a garage in Reno and back to a "bawdy" house, located in the Chicago slums.

Similarly, the FBI picked up the rumor travelling along the underworld grapevine that Dillinger and Nelson were together again. They had met by prearrangement in Kentucky and renewed their alliance. A known contact of the gang furnished another lead. The Dillinger crowd had been seen at a resort operated by a "shady" citizen of the underworld in Fox River Grove, Illinois. Rumor had it that the Barker-Karpis gang had also been sheltered there during their flight from the G-Men. They descended on Fox River Grove. Too late. The gang had fled.

Entrance to the Little Bohemia lodge raided by FBI agents on the evening of April 22, 1934, in an attempt to apprehend the Dillinger gang.

THE RAID ON LITTLE BOHEMIA

On April 22, shortly after noon, another "tip" reached the FBI. The Dillinger gang with their paramours were located at a summer resort in Wisconsin called the Little Bohemia Lodge. Shortly before dusk on the same day, a plane landed at Rhinelander, Wisconsin. A group of Agents stepped out. But disheartening news greeted them. Word had been received that the gang was planning to leave the resort that evening. Plans for a raid at dawn were instantly discarded. The time to attack was now.

Renting the town's antiquated and only available cars, Agents proceeded to drive the fifty miles to Little Bohemia. Two of the cars broke down on the way. Crowding into the remaining cars, they drove on.

As the cars turned into the lane, leading to the resort, headlights were extinguished. Dogs, however, stationed around the grounds, announced their arrival with shrill yelps.

The men of the FBI swarmed out of the cars and made their way on foot toward the brilliantly-lit lodge. They surrounded it in front and on both sides. According to information they had received, a lake to the rear of the lodge, cut off escape from that quarter.

South side of the Little Bohemia lodge showing window and roof used in escape. One man was seen to drop from the roof near the double glass doors.

But the information was faulty. While Tommy Carroll enthusiastically pumped lead at the "G-Men" from the roof and the "women" screamed hysterically, four men slipped silently out the back of the lodge and along a narrow embankment invisible to the Agents. Dillinger, Nelson, Hamilton and Van Meter, later joined by the panting Carroll, fled into the protective shelter of the woods as Agents stormed the lodge with barrages of machine gun fire and tear gas.

When the fumes lifted, three women were found—Helen Gillis, Marie Conforti and Jean Delaney. The rest of the gang had escaped leaving their "molls" to take the rap.

Road on which Special Agent W. Carter Baum was shot and killed by "Baby Face" Nelson on the night of the Little Bohemia raid. Two other officers—an FBI agent and a constable—were seriously injured at this time by Nelson.

MURDER OF SPECIAL AGENT BAUM

During the firing on the resort Special Agents W. Carter Baum and J. C. Newman, accompanied by a police officer, had been dispatched to a nearby farm house in order to get in touch by phone with additional Agents who had arrived in Rhinelander by car.

Driving up the highway they noticed a small, low car with its lights on, parked near the farm house. As the Agents stopped their automobile, a man darted out from the left side of the parked car and confronted them with an automatic. It was "Baby Face" Nelson. Holding the gun even with the door, four inches away from the car, he shouted, "I know you have bullet-proof vests on. I'll shoot you in the head. Get out of that car."

As Agent Newman stepped off the running board of the car and reached for his gun, Nelson turned on him, snarling. "I'll kill you." The automatic barked.

Newman dropped; the bullet, striking him in the forehead, knocked him semi-conscious.

**Special Agent W. Carter Baum who was killed by "Baby Face" Nelson
during the Little Bohemia raid. At the time of his death Agent Baum was
29 years of age, married and the father of two children.**

Simultaneously, the killer turned his gun on the other two officers, alighting from the car. Agent Baum crumpled to the ground instantly killed and the Constable slumped over, severely wounded.

Seizing the officer's car, Nelson drove off wildly into the night.

The brutal slaying of Agent Baum and the serious injuries sustained by the other two officers fanned public sentiment into a blaze. Dillinger, Nelson and their colleagues must be caught. The FBI's search for the desperados became a nationwide manhunt as local law enforcement agencies throughout the country pooled their forces with those of the Federal government in an all out effort to wipe out the Dillinger plague.

DILLINGER BURIES JOHN HAMILTON

Death also followed the Dillinger gang in their flight from the "G-Men." On the day following the Bohemia Raid, police officers near South St. Paul, Minnesota, engaged John Dillinger, Homer Van Meter and John Hamilton in a running gun battle. Although the fugitives escaped, John Hamilton was badly wounded.

Dillinger rushed him to Chicago. Lodging his fallen henchman in a Chicago saloon, he appealed for help through the crime syndicate. But the underworld turned thumbs down. Dillinger was advised to take his buddy and leave town immediately. They were too "hot."

The fugitive contacted the Barker-Karpis gang's physician, Dr. Joseph Moran. The "good doctor," not being on friendly terms with Dillinger at the time, refused to render any aid.

Desperately, Dillinger turned to the Barker-Karpis gang—also on the underworld's black list because of too much "G" heat. "Doc" Barker came to the rescue and offered shelter. But lack of medical attention had aggravated Hamilton's wounds. Gangrene set in. He grew steadily worse. Ten days after the Bohemia Raid, he died.

A hasty conference was held by Dillinger and the Barker-Karpis gang. A burial place had to be decided upon fast. Hamilton dead was a "hot" corpse. A grave was agreed upon—a gravel pit, six miles south of Aurora, Illinois. John Hamilton was buried that evening; his funeral cortege included John Dillinger, Homer Van Meter, Volney Davis, "Doc" Barker, William Weaver and Harry Campbell. Lye was poured over his face to prevent identification in case the body was ever found.

Gravel pit near Oswego, Illimois, in which the body of John Hamilton was found by Special Agents of the FBI on August 28, 1935. Examination of the body revealed a large bullet hole in the back which had ruptured the spinal column but had not penetrated it.

DILLINGER "BUYS" A NEW FACE

With their dead companion safely buried, Dillinger and Van Meter returned to Chicago. The underworld czars had relented and lifted the "ban" somewhat. They sent out "feelers" for Nelson and the rest of the gang to join them as soon as possible.

Meanwhile, they hid out in the home of James Probasco, an ex-convict, in Chicago. Their host received $35 a day for his hospitality. But John Dillinger soon grew restless. He liked people, good times, movies, dancing. There was nothing he could do now but remain in hiding, playing poker with Van Meter and pacing the floor. On occasions when he could stand the suppression no longer, he burst out of the house as soon as night fell. After roaming dark streets for hours he returned weary.

Probasco worried about Dillinger's night walks. He consulted Louis P. Piquette, Dillinger's crooked attorney. The lawyer offered sage advice. "You've gotta get a new face, John. You can't keep going out like that if you don't. People will recognize you. Probasco will get in trouble and I'll lose my best client. Now, I know of a doc...."

Dillinger agreed to a new face. Piquette secured the services of a Dr. William Loeser, a parole violator for a Federal Narcotics conviction. Dr. Bernard Cassidy, another Chicago physician, was engaged to act as a male nurse.

Top: Dillinger's attorney, Louis P. Piquette, who arranged for the facial operations, was convicted of harboring charges.

Bottom: Dr. William Loeser was convicted of harboring Dillinger, and was returned to the United States Penitentiary in Leavenworth.

The operation took place in Probasco's home. It cost John Dillinger $5,000 and almost his life. Cassidy nervously administered too much ether. Dillinger stopped breathing. For several seconds, Van Meter, Probasco, Piquette and Cassidy stared helplessly at the still face. They called frantically to Loeser who had been washing his hands in the bathroom. Seizing his instruments, Dr. Loeser applied emergency treatment.

Death was cheated at that moment. The doctor's quick action restored life to Dillinger. He gasped and began to breathe slowly. The operation proceeded but only local anesthetics were administered.

Several days later, Van Meter submitted to similar "face-lifting." The price was the same—$5000. Included with it was the crude mutilation of the finger bulbs of both Van Meter and Dillinger in an unsuccessful attempt to destroy their fingerprints.

While convalescing in Probasco's home, Dillinger received disheartening news. Pat Cherrington, former girlfriend of John Hamilton, had been seized by the FBI and sentenced to two years. The "G-Men" had also picked up Pat Reilly, the St. Paul bootlegger who had run errands for the gang. He had received a year and a month in a Federal penitentiary and a fine of $2,500.

Still more dismaying was the news about Tony Carroll. Carroll was dead. He had been killed by the police while resisting arrest. Jean Delaney had been with him at the time. She had been sentenced to one year in prison.

Dillinger vowed that as soon as his operation healed, he would restore order to his disintegrating forces. "Baby Face" Nelson was contacted. He agreed to meet Dillinger and Van Meter in front of a schoolhouse on the outskirts of Chicago.

On June 29, 1934, the meeting took place. While one of Nelson's mobsters patrolled the highway, armed with a machine gun, the remnants of the Dillinger gang discussed what was to be their last undertaking together.

They struck the next day in South Bend, Indiana. Dillinger, carrying a "tommy" gun, led seven men into the Merchants National Bank. They seized $28,000, left one dead police officer, and two wounded bystanders.

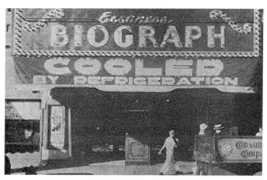

The Biograph Theater in Chicago, Illinois, where John Dillinger spent the last hours of his life seeing a gangster picture "Manhattan Melodrama" with two women companions on the night of July 22, 1934.

THE DEATH OF JOHN DILLINGER

But death was trailing John Dillinger as he headed back to Chicago to celebrate. With his mole and dimples removed, hair dyed black and a mustache, he was confident that he could mingle safely in crowded Chicago without fear of detection.

Dillinger looked for a woman to help him spend his share of the loot. He found not one but two—a Chicago waitress and the keeper of a house of ill-repute. They embarked on an exhilarating round of nightlife—movies, dancing, night clubs.

On a warm Sunday evening, July 22, 1934, Dillinger decided to take his two companions to see the latest gangster picture at the neighborhood theater called, "Manhattan Melodrama."

The women chatted pleasantly as Dillinger drove the car rapidly through the darkened streets. Parking a block from the Biograph Theater, they proceeded to walk toward the brilliantly-illuminated marquee. Other late arrivers fell in behind them. It was almost nine o' clock.

Dillinger chose seats down front. His women companions sat on each side. For an hour and a half, they watched with rapt attention as Clark Gable portrayed the ruthless gangster, bucking the law and finally meeting death in the electric chair.

At ten-thirty, the doors of the theater swung open. Crowds of movie patrons shuffled out into the warm, sticky night. In groups of twos and threes they sauntered idly down Lincoln Avenue, chatting excitedly about the film.

At length, Dillinger, his straw hat set jauntily on his head and trailed slightly by his companions, emerged and began walking down the Avenue.

A man, standing slightly apart from the thinning crowd at the theater's entrance, struck a match and lit a cigar.

That was the signal....

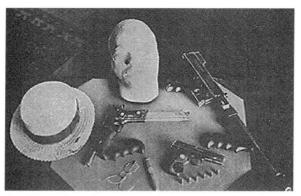

**The death mask and personal belongings of John Dillinger
exhibited at FBI headquarters.**

Acting on a "tip" that John Dillinger would attend the Biograph Theater that evening, FBI Agents had waited patiently for the appearance of their quarry. The lit cigar meant Dillinger had been positively identified. The crude plastic surgery on which he based his anonymity had proved a frail mask, easily shattered under the observing eyes of the FBI.

Instantly, Special Agents and members of the East Chicago, Indiana, police force, under the leadership of Inspector Samuel Cowley, began closing in on all sides. Dillinger, apparently unaware of their approach, continued walking toward his car.

Suddenly, he hesitated, glancing swiftly over his shoulder.

Dillinger began to run and his hand automatically reached for his gun. He turned into the protective darkness of an alley. They were behind him.

The fugitive raised his gun to fire. Several shots rang out. Dillinger gasped and collapsed on the walk—a bullet through his head and two in his chest.

Agents turned the gangster over on his back and gazed soberly down at the still features. John Dillinger, notorious public enemy, who had crammed a lifetime of crime into fifteen short months, was dead.

Lester M. Gillis

Alias "Baby Face" Nelson

WANTED
$5,000.00 REWARD

AUTO THEFT
ROBBERY
BOOTLEGGING
MURDER

LESTER M. GILLIS

The year 1934 was significant in FBI Annals for it marked the conclusion of the kaleidoscopic careers of some of the most notorious "public enemies" of the day. By the end of July, four of the Dillinger gang had met death while resisting arrest—Tommy Carroll, Eddie Green, "Red" Hamilton, John Dillinger.

With the demise of Dillinger the FBI spotlight focused on the remaining fugitives at large—Homer Van Meter, John Chase and "Baby Face" Nelson.

In 1934 Federal Fugitive George "Baby Face" Nelson was a five-foot-four, one hundred and thirty-five-pound bundle of dynamite. The sight of any law enforcement officer, particularly a "G-Man," acted on him like a detonator. His slate-colored eyes would darken with hatred and his gun-hand would come into a "quick-draw" position.

BACKGROUND ON "BABY FACE NELSON"

Nelson, contrary to popular opinion, did not achieve notoriety overnight through mere association with John Dillinger. George Nelson was a polished professional in crime long before he joined the ranks of the Dillinger gang.

His criminal career dated back to his youth in Chicago. It was there under his birth name—Lester Joseph Gillis—that he served his underworld apprenticeship.

By the time Lester Gillis was fourteen, he had mastered the technique of car theft. Dubbed "Baby Face" by his gang due to his juvenile appearance, he ventured to try out his technique.

But the local authorities halted him abruptly. The fourteen-year-old Gillis was convicted of a car robbery and placed in a home for boys in 1922.

Released on parole two years later, he plunged back into his former "light-fingered" habits. Less than five months after his release, he was returned to the "Home" on a similar charge of car theft.

Gillis was placed on probation ten months later. Again he returned to his chosen profession. And again, the law caught up with him. Gillis became the reform school's "star boarder" for another twelve months.

On June 11, 1926, he was released on parole for the third time. Assuming the name, George "Baby Face" Nelson, he determined to acquire a more versatile knowledge of illegal rackets. At 18, Nelson had progressed from tire stealing to running stills and bootlegging. The liquor racket netted him quite a profit until one of his associates, hired to cook mash, stole most of the alcohol.

Quitting the liquor racket, Nelson turned to stick-ups, specializing in armed robbery. He was quite successful for a short while and engineered a series of profitable holdups.

By June of 1931, 23-year-old "Baby Face" Nelson was a veteran crook. His early adolescent appearance had long since been replaced by the slick, hard shell of the cheap Chicago thug. And the bane of his crooked existence—coppers!

But as before, the law caught up with Nelson once more. Convicted on a robbery charge he was sentenced to one year to life in the Illinois State Penitentiary.

A BREAK FOR FREEDOM

Prison life with its many restrictions did not hold any interest for the aspiring Nelson. Seven months after his imprisonment, February of 1932, while being returned to the Illinois Penitentiary after standing trial in Wheaton, Illinois for another robbery charge and receiving an additional sentence of from one year to life, he broke loose.

As the taxicab neared the prison gates, "Baby Face" Nelson pulled a gun, smuggled to him during the trial, on the prison guard and forced him to unlock his handcuffs.

Then sticking the gun into the taxicab driver's back, Nelson ordered him to drive on. On the outskirts of Chicago both guard and driver were shoved out of the car and George Nelson took over the wheel. His destination—Reno, Nevada.

Mrs. Helen Gillis, wife of "Baby Face" Nelson, who shared in her
husband's criminal career until his death.

Joined by his nineteen-year-old wife, Helen Gillis, and their young
son, Nelson sought refuge with the "king pin" of the Reno underworld.
The latter received them warmly and was lavish in his hospitality.

Shortly thereafter, Mr. and Mrs. "Baby Face," bearing a letter of
introduction indorsed by the Reno "big shot," set out for San Francisco.

There the "introductory note" provided Nelson with an open
sesame into a liquor smuggling gang. The roll call of the gang read
like a San Francisco police line-up—Anthony "Soap" Mareno,
Louis Tambini, Joseph "Fatso" Negri and John Paul Chase.

John Paul Chase, close associate of Nelson, apprehended on
December 27, 1934.

JOHN CHASE AND NELSON—FRIENDS IN CRIME

An immediate friendship sprung up between Nelson and Chase. Thirty-one-year-old John Chase took the youthful desperado under his wing and introduced him to the California crime confederacy as his half-brother. Nelson in turn soon exerted his dominating personality over the illiterate Chase, a typical local hoodlum, whose formal education had consisted of five years of grade school and a post-graduate course in bootlegging and petty racketeering.

While not actively engaged in liquor-running, Nelson acted as a "strong-arm" chauffeur for his Reno pal. He soon made the acquaintance of Reno's crime club and became an honorary member.

In September of 1932, Mrs. "Baby Face" became ill. Nelson was frantic. He realized that a reputable hospital would be dangerous territory for the wife of an escaped convict.

He turned to his underworld pals. They gave him the name of Tobe Williams, head of the Vallejo General Hospital in California. Nelson was tipped off that Williams was a "right guy", who would be glad to take care of Helen. His patients included "Ma" Barker and Alvin Karpis. He was smart too. Had his whole community thinking he was a philanthropist and political leader. Only a chosen few of the underworld were aware of Williams' shady activities and that he was an ex-con like themselves who had served time in Montana for burglary.

Nelson rushed his wife to Vallejo and made the acquaintance of Tobe Williams. It was to be a profitable friendship for Williams and a fortunate one for Nelson. Two years later "Baby Face" Nelson was harbored on several occasions when the G-Men were searching for him by the understanding Williams. Of course the fugitive had to pay plenty for the hospitality but that was expected and unquestioned.

NELSON ENTERTAINS THE DILLINGER GANG

In the spring of 1933, Mr. and Mrs. Nelson returned east. Leaving Chase in control of the bootlegging activities, they journeyed to Indiana. A cottage at Long Beach on Lake Michigan was secured.

The Nelsons held "open house" that summer for their many criminal associates. Included among their weekend guests were four members of the Dillinger gang.

Sociabilitys continued on into the fall. On Thanksgiving day of 1933, Mr. and Mrs. "Baby Face" accompanied by Homer Van Meter and his paramour, Marie Conforti, sat down to a sumptuous dinner at the home of a "hot gun bootlegger", H. S. Lebman, in San Antonio, Texas.

Eleven days later, however, they left San Antonio rather hurriedly. Tommy Carroll on that day, December 11, 1933, had engaged in a gun battle with the local police. Detective H. C. Perrow had been killed in the fray. Lebman, always a gracious host, permitted Carroll to make a change of clothing and effect an escape from his saddlery and harness shop.

The Nelsons proceeded on to San Francisco. There "Baby Face" resumed his association with John Chase and "Fatso" Negri. Shortly after, Helen Gillis became a patient again at the Vallejo General Hospital under the name of Helen Williams. Hospitalized for several weeks, she was visited daily by Nelson and their young son. Unsuspecting fellow patients at the hospital were duly impressed by the charming domestic scene which the Nelsons always created.

MURDER IN MINNEAPOLIS

On January 22, 1934, Nelson bought himself a new getaway car, a Hudson sedan. Nineteen thirty-four California license plates, #6-H-475, were secured and issued to him under the alias, James Rogers.

One month later, the Nelson entourage—Mr. and Mrs. "Baby Face," their sons, Nelson's mother, Mrs. Gillis, and John Chase moved on to Minneapolis, Minnesota. A few days afterward Theodore W. Kidder was shot and killed in Minneapolis. Eye witnesses to the murder observed the killers' car, a Hudson sedan with 1934 California license plate #6-H-475. When the license plate was checked, the name was found to be—James Rogers. The local authorities descended on the Rogers' apartment. Too late.... "Baby Face," his mother, wife, son, and Chase had fled.

UNDERWORLD RUMOR CREDITS NELSON WITH ANOTHER MURDER

Bremerton, Washington, was the destination of the killers as they sped away from Minneapolis. Nelson had a sister living there. He decided to leave his offspring with her until the heat died down.

One week later Nelson, Helen, and Chase arrived in Reno, Nevada. That very night, March 22, 1934, Roy J. Frisch, a cashier for a Reno bank, disappeared and was never seen again.

A rumor trickled out of Reno..."'Baby Face' Nelson got rid of Frisch permanently ... Yeah.... As a favor for the 'Boss'...."

Frisch had been an important government witness in a case involving the prosecution of the Reno "Boss" on a charge of using the mails to defraud.

With his debt to his Reno pal "paid off in full", Nelson accompanied by his wife and Chase hurriedly left Reno that evening and headed for San Francisco. On the following day, "Baby Face" contacted his old crony, "Fatso" Negri.

A crisp one hundred dollar bill pressed in Negri's oily hand sent the chunky racketeer hurrying off to clean up his pals' affairs. In Reno, Negri bustled around securing some clothes left behind in the killers' haste to quit town. He also left Nelson's forwarding address with the underworld clique in case any of the Dillinger gang should wish to contact them.

G-MEN INTERRUPT NELSON'S VACATION AT LITTLE BOHEMIA

Meanwhile George Nelson and Helen Gillis proceeded to drive leisurely back to the midwest. On April 16, 1934, they arrived at the Crystal Ballroom at Fox River Grove, Illinois. There Dillinger, "Red" Hamilton, Van Meter, Tommy Carroll and their concubines were waiting for them.

A conference was called. Nelson and Dillinger agreed that the "G-Heat" was getting too hot for comfort. They all needed a vacation in a spot far removed from the prying nose of the law.

The host of the Crystal Ballroom, a professional harborer of notorious criminals, offered his help. There was a resort in Manitowish, Wisconsin, called the Little Bohemia Lodge. He wrote a letter of introduction for the "boys" to the woman proprietor. Two days later the entire gang set out for their proposed vacation.

They found the Wisconsin lodge secluded, sturdy and sociable. There were plenty of drinks in the bar, poker at night, swimming and dancing during the day. It seemed like a perfect "set up." "Baby Face" Nelson began to relax.

It lasted only two days. G-Men raided the lodge on the evening of April 24. In the ensuing escape, "Baby Face" murdered an FBI Agent and wounded another Agent and a local officer.

His version of the killing as he bragged to his gangster pals was, "I saw some men sitting in an automobile. I got out of my car to ask them directions. When I came closer, I saw they were G-Men. I let them have it. The fellow at the wheel slumped and the fellow who was getting out of the car from the side, I gave him a couple of slugs in the back."

Left: Picture of John Paul Chase secured from his paramour, Sally Backman.

Center: Van Meter's paramour, Marie "Mickey" Conforti, who was sentenced to serve one year in a federal penetentiary.

Right: Joseph Raymond "Fatso" Negri, associate of Nelson, who was convicted of harboring a fugitive.

NELSON FLEES AFTER KILLING G-MAN

The gang split up after the Bohemia Raid. Chase and Carroll "holed in" at Nelson's hideout at Lake Como, Wisconsin. They were joined shortly afterwards by Helen Gillis and Jean Delaney. The women, abandoned by the gang during the raid, had been apprehended. After pleading guilty to the indictment charging them with harboring Dillinger and Carroll, they had received probationary sentences. As soon as they were released, they had headed back to rejoin their men.

The remainder of the gang—Dillinger, Hamilton and Van Meter had proceeded to Chicago. Contact between the two factions was carried on via the underworld grapevine.

But as the FBI continued its concentrated manhunt for the fugitives, disturbing news began to trickle in from the underground route to Nelson. Former friends, contacts, harborers were being surveilled on a 24-hour basis by the G-men. The crime confederacies in Chicago, Reno, and St. Paul were being blasted open by the "G-heat." G-men were closing in everywhere. Nelson found the price for bed, board and anonymity daily rising to stupendous heights.

On June 7, 1934, Tommy Carroll and Jean Delaney quit the Lake Como hideout. They headed for Waterloo, Iowa. Death was waiting there for Carroll. Ordered to surrender by local police, Carroll had pulled his gun. The police fired. Officers lifted the sobbing Jean Delaney away from the gangster's lifeless body sprawled on the street.

Returned to Wisconsin, Jean Delaney's probation was revoked and she was sentenced to one year and a day in a federal penitentiary.

The news of Carroll's death enflamed the twisted mind of "Baby Face" Nelson. He momentarily considered descending on Waterloo and "getting the copper who got Carroll." But the instinct of self-preservation was too strong. It cautioned prudence.

Burrowing even deeper in his hideout, the enraged Nelson called a hasty conference with Chase. Funds were running low. Money had to be obtained fast. Dillinger was contacted. "A reunion in Chicago? Right...."

On June 29, 1934, Nelson, Dillinger, Chase and Van Meter met. The next day they robbed the South Bend, Indiana bank.

Nelson and Chase parted from Dillinger and Van Meter jubilantly. They were $13,000.00 richer.

Homer Van Meter, member of the Dillinger gang and associate of Nelson, killed while resisting arrest by St. Paul police officers on August 23, 1934.

THE G-HEAT GETS HOTTER

Picking up Helen Gillis, Nelson and Chase set out for the west coast. It was a slow, tortuous trip. Driving by night, brief respites at highway tourist cabins, indigestible meals snatched in road houses, a constant gnawing suspicion of all strangers. "Baby Face" Nelson was beginning to find out just how warm the "G-Heat" could be.

It was in one of the many nondescript cabins while en route that Nelson heard the radio flash on the night of July 22, 1934. "John Dillinger was killed by FBI Agents this evening while resisting arrest.... Inspector Sam Cowley who successfully conducted the manhunt for Dillinger, has been appointed by J. Edgar Hoover, Director of the FBI, to carry on the hunt for Lester Gillis, alias George "Baby Face" Nelson...."

A cold chill swept over Nelson leaving him trembling. His wife stared at him with frightened eyes. Chase leaned over and snapped the radio off.

"Let's go," Nelson muttered. "We'll sleep in the car later."

It was time to move again—to travel in an aimless pattern over the back roads of the West constantly weaving, dodging, retracing routes.

Jack Perkins, friend of Nelson, was one of seventeen persons indicted on charges of harboring Nelson. He was sentenced to two years in a federal penitentiary.

A friend of the Nelsons was picked up along the way—Jack Perkins. He brought along his wife and three-year-old son. Domesticity was Nelson's idea. The men wore light-colored inexpensive trousers and soft white shirts open at the neck. The women—cotton house dresses and short leather jackets. The Perkins baby was lulled to sleep on the back seat among the vast arsenal of tommy guns, rifles, pistols, bullet proof vests and ammunition. No one looked twice at the carload of passengers with the smiling baby as the group covered the states of California and Nevada during the summer of 1934.

On August 23, 1934, more bad news reached Nelson. Homer Van Meter had been killed on that day while resisting arrest by St. Paul Police officers. As Nelson savagely drove the dust covered car down the highway, his mind was flaming with the desire to "get those coppers." But again—caution overrode his impetuousness. He vented his thwarted rage on his passengers—Helen, Chase and the obliging Perkins.

On August 29, 1934, the Perkins family departed from the fugitives and Sally Backman, Chase's concubine from Sausalito, California, joined them.

Again, they set out. Their rambling itinerary included California, Nevada, Colorado, Kansas.... Reaching St. Charles, Illinois, on September 10, John Chase and his sweetheart parted with the Nelsons temporarily. While Mr. and Mrs. "Baby Face" remained hidden in Illinois, John Chase and Sally Backman spent a short interlude in New York City. While there, Chase, under an assumed name, bought an Airflow DeSoto sedan to use on the return trip West. Two days later Sally Backman departed by plane for San Francisco. Her purpose—to destroy some old photographs of Chase she had left at home before the G-Men found them.

But she arrived too late. By painstakingly sifting all information on Nelson's colleague, FBI Agents had uncovered the name of his paramour and secured the pictures.

Meanwhile John Chase drove his new car to California via Helena, Montana. At Helena he contacted a friend who rented a safety deposit box for him. Chase placed $2,000 in the box, giving the keys to the friend.

He proceeded on to Reno and on October 10, 1934, rejoined the Nelsons and "Fatso" Negri. A Reno garage operator, Frank Cochran, arranged the meeting between Chase and Nelson. From Reno the entourage travelled to Hot Springs, Nevada, remaining there a week.

"Baby Face" Nelson and John Paul Chase. This is the only known picture of the fugitives taken together.

On October 24, 1934, Chase bought a Ford pick-up truck. A few days later, the fugitives with Helen Gillis piled into it and set out for their old stamping grounds—Chicago.

But the sands of time were running out for them. The G-Men under the zealous leadership of Inspector Samuel P. Cowley were countering the mobility of Nelson with a flexibility of investigative technique. Hourly, reports on all leads, tips and rumors embracing the nationwide manhunt for the fugitives, flooded the Chicago Field Office. There they were sorted, assembled and carefully checked by Inspector Cowley.

On the afternoon of November 27, 1934, one such lead made its way into the Chicago Office. A man resembling George "Baby Face" Nelson had been seen in the vicinity of Lake Geneva, Wisconsin, that day. With him were another man and a woman.

Immediately, all Agents, covering leads in the Chicago vicinity, were alerted....

THE END OF THE TRAIL

"Baby Face" was driving that afternoon, Helen beside him and John Chase in the rear. They were on the way to Chicago to meet "Fatso."

As Nelson sent the car speeding down the Northwest Highway, he noticed an automobile approach and pass them. He stared at its occupants suspiciously.

"G-Men!"

Nelson thrilled with sadistic anticipation as he deftly manipulated the car in a sharp turn until it fell in behind the Bureau car.

Recognizing the fugitives in the car following them as Nelson and Chase, the two FBI men, who had been out covering a routine lead, raced their car down the highway with Nelson in hot pursuit. But the odds were against the "G-Men." Chase was firing a rifle at them from the rear of the car. They could only retaliate with pistol fire.

A bullet from one of the Agent's guns struck Nelson's motor. It slowed down and began to lose speed. Hoping to spread the alarm and secure additional manpower and firearms, the Agents sped away to the nearest town.

But in the meantime, acting on the latest tip that Nelson had left Lake Geneva and was heading toward Chicago, Inspector Cowley and Agent Hollis had taken to the main highway hoping to intercept the fugitive.

As they passed Nelson's car going in the opposite direction they recognized the occupants. Swinging their car around, the Agents sped after them.

The two cars raced along the highway. It was late afternoon. The road ahead was a smooth, unbroken pattern. There was no traffic. To the men of the FBI following closely behind the fugitives the task of apprehension was a perilous one. They realized Nelson would not submit without a fight. Backed up by his wife and Chase, he would be a snarling killer. It was too late now to call for additional Agents. Cowley and Hollis determined to do their utmost to apprehend their man.

But at that moment, Nelson suddenly swung his car off the main highway on to a side road and stopped abruptly. While Hollis vainly struggled to swing in behind the fugitive's car, Nelson, Chase and Helen Gillis jumped out of the car. By the time the Bureau car had skidded up the highway almost 150 feet and stopped, Nelson and Chase had taken up positions behind their car. Helen Gillis was lying prone in a nearby field.

As Cowley and Hollis began to step out of their car, Nelson raked them with a volley of machine gun fire. Chase backed him up with rifle fire.

Both Agents immediately fell to the highway badly wounded. Although torn with bullets, they turned their guns on Nelson. They continued firing until through their rapidly-dimming vision they saw Nelson stagger and clutch his stomach.

As Nelson slumped to the ground, Chase picked up the machine gun and turned it on the "G-Men." There was little return fire this time. Agent Hollis lay dead—Inspector Cowley, dying.

Seizing the Bureau car, Chase and Nelson, supported by his wife, drove rapidly away.

The Bureau car driven by Special Agent Hollis and Inspector Cowley on November 27, 1934. Seized by the fugitives after their gun battle with the agents, it carried the dying Nelson to his last hideout. After Nelson's death, Chase abandoned the car in Illinois.

CONCLUSION

Inspector Cowley died in the Elgin Hospital in Barrington, Illinois, during the early morning hours of November 28, 1934.

On the same day the body of George "Baby Face" Nelson, stripped of clothing and wrapped in a blanket, was located in a ditch on the side of a road in Niles City, Illinois. The bullets fired from the guns of Inspector Cowley and Agent Hollis had taken their toll. Seventeen slugs were found in his body.

Helen Gillis was apprehended by FBI Agents the following day. Returned to Wisconsin, she was placed in a Federal Penitentiary for violating her probation.

The final chapter on the Dillinger gang was recorded on December 27, 1934, when Nelson's partner in crime, John Paul Chase, was taken into custody at Mount Shasta, California. On March 25, 1935, Chase, after being tried and found guilty of the murder of Inspector Cowley, was sentenced to spend the rest of his life in the Federal penitentiary at Alcatraz.

Inspector Samuel P. Cowley. At the time of his death on November 28, 1934, he was 35 years of age, married, and the father of two children.

Special Agent Herman E. Hollis. At the time of his death he was 31 years old, married and the father of one child.

At the Washington headquarters of the FBI, two more names were inscribed on the large bronze plaque honoring the memory of men like Cowley and Hollis who died in the service of their country.

Index

Made in the USA
San Bernardino, CA
02 January 2019